PRAISE FOR
DATING THE GATEKEEPER

"My reps are so excited about the response to the 'Dating the Gatekeeper' technique that they are calling me laughing about how well their cold calls have gone."

— *Todd Farris, Sales Manager, Tennessee*

"After we tried 'Dating the Gatekeeper' together in the field, I decided to use my old method on a few cold calls to compare the responses. I got rejected immediately. I will be using your technique from now on!"

— *Mark Kremer, Experienced Sales Representative, Texas*

"By incorporating the 'Dating the Gatekeeper' strategies into our sales culture, our dealership experienced immediate and long standing success that is still going strong today!"

— *Joe Breczka, General Manager, New York*

"There is no doubt Tom's 'Dating the Gatekeeper' philosophy and approach delivers results. Initially, our sales team was resistant to trying something so 'weird' and 'time-consuming' in their view. However, once the program got rolling, things changed significantly. The Team actually looked forward to cold calling and really enjoyed the reactions they got from the prospects they met. Results? Oh yeah. The sales team won (and kept) at least one new customer, every day, for an entire year! If you don't use Tom's 'Dating the Gatekeeper' program to grow your business, your replacement will."

— *Brennan Thomson, Sales and Marketing Director,*
Calgary, Alberta

DATING
the GATEKEEPER

Successful Cold Calling Without Fear or Failure

by
Tom Buxton

DATING
the GATEKEEPER

Illumify Media Group
www.IllumifyMedia.com
"We Make Your Writing Shine"

Print: 978-1-947360-02-0
eBook: 978-1-947360-03-7

CONTENTS

SHOULD YOU READ THIS BOOK?

So, why would anyone write another book about sales when so many good, bad, and downright out-of-touch sales books already exist?

And why should you spend your valuable time reading another sales book when you could update your Facebook account or take a snooze?

If you are looking for techniques to make the fastest sale or hone your manipulation skills, this book is definitely not for you. If you are already a high-powered salesperson and close most of the business that you call on, enjoy your siesta with my compliments.

Alternatively, if cold calling and the frequent rejection it guarantees makes you lose sleep at night, if the word *relationship* inspires you more than the word *close,* if you are afraid of being replaced by an online marketplace like Amazon, or, if you work in sales because you like helping people and making money, you need this book.

Life truly is a sales job, and over the past nearly forty years, I have experienced extreme success at the "game." It's not without hard work though. I have studied numerous sales books and participated in, taught, and modeled various techniques from Professional Selling Skills, Sandler, and Strategic Selling seminars. Yet my heart aches whenever I run across dedicated people with excellent training that fail at this honorable profession.

Why is failure so frequent among salespeople? Moreover, how can sales managers find ways to minimize the washout rate of the people they lead? These are the gut-wrenching challenges that inspired me to write this book.

INTRODUCTION

"What will it take to get you into that car today?"

If you're comfortable with this sort of question, *Dating the Gatekeeper* is not for you. On the other hand, if you love establishing positive relationships and making more money selling to people who enjoy working with you, read on.

My wife, Jenny, and I were celebrating our two daughters moving out of our home for the final time (we hope!). So, we decided to replace the four-door mélange (yes, that is a color) sedan she had driven for years. I was in charge of researching and arranging the initial contacts. Jenny was the ultimate decision maker who could overrule any idea or model of car that I chose. I knew that the car needed to be

1. Good looking,
2. Two doors rather than four,
3. Fast or at least very quick, and
4. Include a manual rather than automatic transmission.

Money wasn't the main issue, but it was important enough that I decided to look at used cars rather than new. Almost immediately I discovered two cars that I thought would please the decision maker. A somewhat notorious dealership in Denver that sold new and used American cars advertised the first car; the second was offered at an Audi showroom.

After showing Jenny photos of both cars, she decided to visit the dealerships with me the next day. To somewhat protect us from the tension I was certain would arise at the first dealership, I scheduled a meeting with the Internet sales manager. It turned out to be a strategic move on our part, because the pressure was intense from the moment we arrived.

Balloons and a myriad of salespeople greeted us from the street. As soon as we had parked, sales associates opened both of our doors. Behind them stood more beaming salespeople who fixed their eyes on Jenny, because she is much more attractive than me.

"What sort of car are you looking to buy today?"

Jenny looked at me with a mixture of fear and confusion. Did we really want to buy anything from people like them? She didn't know the answer to their questions, but they continued to ask her.

"Excuse me, ma'am. What sort of car are you looking to buy today?"

"Ask him," she replied, looking at me. "He knows why we're here."

"We have an appointment with the Internet manager to drive a car," I said.

The mood of the sales people changed quickly, as if all the balloons in the parking lot had just been exposed to an extremely cold blast of air. They obviously hated being replaced by sales methods they didn't understand and couldn't control.

The Internet sales manager was younger than the rest of the salespeople. In fact he looked like he was twelve years old. Sadly, he had already learned some tactics from his older associates. Jenny drove the car while he coiled his lanky frame into the small back seat and started to ask me questions.

"What do you think of the car and are you looking for financing?" I couldn't tell yet whether or not the decision-maker liked the car, but I knew that she didn't like being asked questions while she was driving.

He tried to pick up cues from my wife as well, but she was busy making sure she didn't destroy someone else's car. So he came back to me with an offshoot of that famous close: "Do you like the car enough that you would like to take it home today?"

I looked at Jenny and I knew immediately—thirty plus years of marriage will do that to you—she didn't like the car much and had already determined she couldn't trust the dealer enough to look at anything else they had. We needed to escape the situation. Thank Heaven I kept the keys to the car we had parked in their lot!

As always, she was very polite and replied, "It isn't exactly what I am looking for, but I'll consider it after I drive some other cars."

Her last phrase gave our salesman a small (almost microscopic) opening, so he jumped right through it.

"We have a great number of other sports cars on our lot. I'm sure that one of them will be just right."

We all knew they had nothing that came close to the specifications of the German sports car she drove, but he had to try, right?

Wrong! He should have learned when to cut his losses. Instead, the decision-maker now definitely was not going to buy a car from this gentleman or the dealership. That didn't stop him and the newly reinflated sales people from escorting us to our car, while pointing out other "fantastic deals" and offering to significantly lower the price of the vehicle she had driven.

To tell you the truth, I'm not sure how we were finally able to vacate the dealership, but I *am* confident we didn't run over anyone on the way out.

Finally alone, we discussed the incident. My wife, who doesn't experience high-pressure sales on a frequent basis, was almost in tears and felt somewhat sick to her stomach.

"Why does anyone sell like that?" she asked. "Don't they know most people hate it?"

Her question really challenged me. Why do so many men and women sacrifice their normal personalities in order to close the sale? Don't they know they will lose creditability and ultimately most of their prospects by being so pushy?

I had little hope for my chosen profession as we drove to the second car dealer. I was pretty sure my wife didn't want to subject herself to another horrible experience that day, but I did my best to assure her the next dealership *had* to be different.

It was! We parked in the lot and no one accosted us with questions about what we needed. We walked over to the car she selected for us to examine—and we weren't attacked. In fact, I found myself becoming a bit annoyed that we had to walk all the way to the showroom floor to find a salesperson.

Entering the main door, two younger men dressed in khakis and golf shirts greeted us. They asked us how they could be of assistance, and they even offered us something to drink and eat before we got started. (By the way, I think that the other dealership advertised they were serving hot dogs, but we were never given a second to consider whether we wanted one.) We weren't thirsty or hungry, but we *were* intrigued. *When are they going to jump on us with high pressure tactics?* we thought. *Are they let just the two of us drive their car, since the back seat was too small for anyone else to fit in?*

We had our answers soon enough. Once they determined what car we were considering, they asked if we wanted to take it for a test drive. "Yes, we would like to drive the car," we said. After making copies of our insurance information and drivers licenses, they gave us the keys.

The moment she saw it, Jenny pictured it as hers. That presented a separate problem from our most recent experience. How would I negotiate a fair deal for a car that my wife adored? We also liked the young salesmen who worked with us. They were polite and clean cut and handsome. *Perhaps one of them would be a good match for one of our two daughters*, we thought. Then we came to our senses and decided that we would not tell them the extent to which Jenny loved the car, or about our daughters. The sales manager appeared when we returned and tried to close the deal, but we felt too boxed in by his arguments about how special the car was.

"It's the only model in Denver," he claimed, which turned out to be true.

"Yes," I argued. "But I know for a fact that this car has been sitting on the lot for over a month!" I had done my research too. Very few people want a car with a stick shift. He offered a price. We rejected his price and offered a lower one. He held to his price. We said no. We left.

Three days later they called us and offered us the price that they had considered so unfair when we first visited. We reviewed the situation and decided to buy the car based on three reasons:

1. My wife loved the car and there weren't any others like it,

2.   The young men had been so courteous and "non-salesy" during our visit, and

3.   The price was not the lowest possible but fair.

Even though we purchased the car, we didn't like the game they forced us to play in order to buy it. We wanted the deal to be win-win all the way through. Had the sales manager at the second dealership been reasonable about his price the first day, we probably would have bought the car right then. He lost hundreds of dollars for his company because he was determined to win, rather than compromise with us. If a similar car had been available in town, we would have tried to purchase *it* rather than deal with him again.

Is it possible that selling collaboratively (win-win) actually results in better relationships and higher profits? My answer is an unqualified "YES!"

This book is for sales people who, like me, hate the "always be closing" mantra that has been foisted upon our profession. I want to be known as a sales professional who loves people and provides a valuable product or service, rather than another one of those jerks who manipulate people for a living.

I hope you will be challenged and encouraged

> Strive to be known as a sales professional who loves people and provides a valuable product or service.

by reading *Dating the Gatekeeper*. The book's goal is to create successful sales opportunities by doing the exact opposite of what most sales people are taught. Rather than finding ways to get around the Gatekeeper, *Dating the Gatekeeper* emphasizes their importance to any successful sales process. The chapters are arranged in such a way as to highlight the challenges of gaining new business using the techniques that are currently in vogue. They are followed by an in-depth discussion of cold calling that emphasizes relationship building and win/win sales techniques.

In chapter 1, we will consider the difficulty in being an effective salesperson while maintaining a moral compass. In chapters 2 and 3 we examine prospective buyers and how pushy sales people affect them. In the chapter 4, we explore the alternate reality of selling for the benefit of your prospect *and* yourself. Cold calling is the most difficult task any salesperson must accomplish, so in chapter 5 we will look at a reliable method that I still use to minimize rejection. Chapter 6 describes a simple process that will open the way for you to meet with the decision maker. Have you ever wondered why prospect meetings can go so bad, so quickly? Chapters 7 and 8 answer that question and provide you with a specific "unsales plan," including next steps. In chapter 9, we discuss the fact that under the right circumstances, salespeople should be decide whether to choose a customer, rather than the other way around. The last chapter is my favorite because I am passionate about helping everyone who desires to sell to do so in a manner that is honest and relational.

If a kinder and more effective sales methodology sounds intriguing to you, please join me as we explore the possibilities of dating the Gatekeeper.

CHAPTER 1

UNLEARNING YOUR ABCs

What is your favorite form of rejection?

A. "We're happy with our current vendor (supplier, product, service, etc)."

B. "If you don't leave immediately I'll call security!"

C. "Please leave a voicemail, and I'll call you right back." (This was your thirteenth call to the prospect and every time it yields the same response.)

D. "I'm too busy to talk to you and please don't call back."

E. *Click* [Dial tone]

F. All of the Above (If you *like* them, you're probably a sociopath.)

G. None of the Above (I'll bet you went into sales because you love building relationships.)

COMPANIES HIRE RELATIONSHIP-BUILDERS BUT SET THEM UP TO FAIL

Many executives think that salespeople are overpaid and underworked narcissists. Maybe some are, but in my years of selling I have discovered that depression rather than narcissism is their most common malady. This is especially true when the salesperson values relationships and is passionate about making a positive difference for their customers as well as the company for which they work.

Companies hire salespeople based on their ability to create a first impression. If the prospective hire speaks clearly, seems organized, and appears crazy enough to apply for the job converting prospects to customers (cold calling), they are often hired on the spot! If you asked the hiring coordinator why they took a chance on someone they hardly knew, often you will hear them say, "It seemed like they could build great relationships."

However, the same company that hires people to build relationships often assumes that the skills that impressed the hiring officer will enable the salesperson to grow business quickly. Product and process training can be quite extensive, but too many companies assume that the sales rep either should know how to approach prospects or that their winsome manner will bring in a stupendous amount of new business. Alas, most companies underestimate the time it will take to build a sales territory. Sales leaders want an immediate return on their investment (ROI) and will fire numerous underlings quickly when they fail to meet their inflated projections.

THE MANIPULATION TRAP

From my nearly forty years of experience in sales of one type or another, just being a nice person doesn't gain customers. Managing calls and prospects successfully from the first day a rep joins a company is the only way to produce a winning sales culture and team. Also, many relationship-oriented salespeople fail to accomplish their basic objective to grow business in industries from selling Aston Martins to Zillow, because companies assume they know how to build relationships in a sales environment. In too many cases they are mistaken, which results in disaster for the salesperson and a lot of turnover for the company.

In response to this tragedy, some companies invest in sales training. Many excellent books and seminars address issues like overcoming objections, up-selling, cross-selling, and asking good questions. However, because of unrealistic expectations, either from the hiring company or the salesperson, many of the great suggestions provided in sales training are sacrificed in the name of getting to the close. In fact, shortening the sales cycle through manipulation and pressure have become pervasive in American sales culture. It originated in a movie that you may have never seen, yet it affects almost every salesperson or team.

This movie, one that I hate, is quoted or emulated more often among salespeople than any other. This is a great shame because in my humble opinion it has permanently damaged the notion of sales, both as an honorable profession and as a genuinely meaningful and satisfying career path.

Glengarry Glen Ross tells the story of a real estate sales team and the manner in which they prospect for new business. In one memorable scene the team participates in a sales contest. The person with the highest sales wins a trip to Hawaii, second place wins a set of steak knives, while the third-place finisher is fired.

As you can imagine, the movie's mood is dark and its moral hard to determine. It's actually a great example of sales satire intended to make fun of the subject by over-dramatizing its faults and making a mockery of the topic it addresses. Too bad so many sales managers and other professionals who should know better have used the movie to teach sales, rather than highlight the brutal excesses that pressure-based sales tactics can cause.

Even if you haven't seen the movie, you have probably heard its most famous line: "A-B-C. A-Always, B-Be, C-Closing. Always be closing. ALWAYS BE CLOSING!" In other words, don't worry about what the prospect says or needs, push them until you gain the sale.

All of us have been tempted to follow this slogan at one time or another. But have you ever asked yourself, *Do I enjoy buying anything from a "pushy" sales person?* My guess is that over 90 percent of you would say "no," and yet A-B-C is still the goal of most sales organizations.

ENDLESS COLD CALLING DOESN'T DO ANYONE ANY GOOD

I have heard sales trainers tell their pupils not to waste time talking to anyone except their "target" to avoid becoming entangled with non-decision makers. "Every moment with company employees," they'll say, "needs to be spent determining how to find and close the decision maker as quickly as possible."

Those sales trainers also advocate making a ridiculous number of cold calls every day, hoping the rep will sell something to one or two of the prospects.

For those who believe in this type of approach, I have two questions: First, what sort of impression are you leaving with the forty to sixty people who won't buy from your company that day? Also, are they more or less likely to buy from your company in the future if the rep annoyed them the first time they met?

One day I was in my office and the phone rang. "Do your reps have any conception of how obnoxious they are?" It was an office manager whom multiple reps from my company visited within a very short period of time. She made the effort to track me down in order to "stop the nonsense." Once she determined that I was responsible for the six separate reps who had called on her company during the previous two weeks, she clearly stated why she would never buy from us. The reps were pushy and obnoxious and insulted her current supplier. And that was why she demanded we never call on her company again.

Now I can hear some of you saying, "Isn't that awesome? Your reps were attacking the opportunities in their market." I couldn't disagree more, because when we stop treating people as individuals, sales reps become insensitive to their prospect's current situation. In most cases, sales growth initiatives singularly focused on generating "numbers" are doomed to fail along with the sales teams that initiate them.

The "Always Be Closing" attitude isn't as effective as it used to be, and it insults the people we are trying to entice. It also damages relationship-oriented sales professionals who fear rejection and take a prospect's anger personally. But, that doesn't stop companies from resorting to such tactics on a regular basis.

One time, our company headquarters wanted to generate higher sales immediately, and they didn't care how we did it, so they mandated blitz calling. This occurred before the advent of centralized customer relationship management (CRM) tools like Salesforce or ProsperWorks, so the reps were told more or less to "go sic'em." They demanded that every rep in the company make at least five to ten cold calls per day—although many of them were already selling over one million dollars of products per year. I figured that if we followed our company directive, our thirty-five local reps would call on every possible target in our region within two weeks. I was not an advocate of this initiative because I had already seen the damage that blitzes can do to prospects and sales professionals. Luckily our sales were already good enough that our division was allowed to postpone the initiative until a later date. That day never came because the mandate died of its own stupidity. But other sales teams within our company were not as fortunate.

Management would say that they didn't intend for the reps' techniques to sink into the gutter, but when you think about it, what should they have expected? Pressures increased while the morale of the sales teams that were forced into this type of sales deteriorated quickly. They were forced to turn up the heat on the clients. High-pressure sales tactics including price-cutting, disparaging the customer's current supplier, and some even outright lied about our company's abilities. How productive was our new initiative? Meager sales growth at very low margins and new accounts that showed no loyalty were the only measurable results. This process resulted in untold damage to the reps who were forced to comply with the directive and minimized the chance of prospects becoming long-term customers.

Does making a ridiculous amount of cold calls help reps build relationships or does it make them afraid to initiate any cold calls at all? What would you guess? Over time, many of our company's seasoned salespeople stopped growing their business. I contend that the pressure to be rabid relators rather than relationship builders destroyed their ability to bring in new business.

The pressure to be rabid relators rather than relationship builders destroyed their ability to bring in new business

RELATIONSHIP-BASED SALES VS COLD CALLING

Nearly every business person I meet asks me the same question: "Where can I find sales professionals who can build relationships and who are willing to cold call?" Guess what? If we try to hire people who can build good relationships, they will perform very poorly at cold calling using the Always Be Closing method.

Because relationship-based sales professionals who can grow business are so hard to find, many companies opt for the hunter-farmer model. This model is dependent on finding people who are comfortable with confrontation and will climb any mountain or, more practically, disrupt fifty people's day in order to find one or two possible "closes."

Are some of these hunters successful? Yes, they may open numerous accounts, but if the track record of one of the largest companies in my industry means anything, their employers need to be prepared for constant turnover. A few years ago an executive from this competitor told me that they hire new hunters to replace those who have resigned or been fired—at a turnover rate of between 60 and 80 percent per year. What does a statistic like that do to a company's culture or an aspiring sales rep's confidence?

People who don't work in sales often assume the wages and freedom representatives enjoy are obscene and that the rep's life involves mostly fine food and golf courses. Reps typically spend very little time behind a desk and do not punch a time clock, so their life must be grand, right?

Some salespeople may have led lives of leisure in the past, but in recent years the landscape has changed dramatically. For many reps, the thrill is gone. Some have brought this trouble on themselves due to their refusal to change. Too many reps spend their time route running, moonlighting, and focusing on just about any other task besides growing their business. Working as a successful rep in today's world is tougher than ever, and in many cases management does little to help them adjust to the cultural change. Since the Great Recession of 2008, businesses have tried to become more efficient or at least cut their investment in full-time employees. This further challenges reps who don't follow a sales process, especially when the prospect or customer is a millennial. We will look at this specific issue more in chapter 4.

When you analyze the challenges that potential customers bring to the sales process, growing an account base can be a very daunting task. Prospects are easier to find but more difficult to connect with than in the past. The Internet has replaced many sales representatives, so unless a sales professional can add lots of value, they become redundant or annoying. So why would anyone want to be a rep?

In the next chapter we will examine why prospects often hate reps and how the "Always Be Closing" mentality frequently leads to sudden and frequent failure.

CHAPTER 2

SHOW UP AND THROW UP

Have you ever felt desperate to get away from a salesperson?

Shortly after reading about a new advancement in cellphones called the Blackberry (yes, I'm *that* old!), one of their sales people left me a message and I agreed to meet. My position in our division made me responsible for the performance of over thirty salespeople, so I was always looking for ways to help them succeed. We met even though I knew that buying smartphones for our entire staff was way above my pay grade. I figured during her sales call she would ask about our situation and my ability to approve such a purchase.

I was wrong.

She began her call with one closed-ended question, "Tom, have you heard of a Blackberry before our meeting today?"

"Yes, and I am intrigued by what it does but can't be completely sure that it will fit my sales rep's needs."

That was all it took to start up the features and benefits engine on her sales machine. She began listing all the ways that sales teams were being positively impacted by the Blackberry and how her product was the only one that would satisfy the need for efficiently sending and receiving e-mails from a remote location through push technology.

"The scroll wheel enables your rep to instantly view their most recent or important emails," she said as she continued to "throw up" on me about other features. "Because the Blackberry 6820 also comes with a fully functional phone (whether it actually was usable as a phone could be debated), your employees will always be connected to customers, other reps, and your sales management team."

She droned on and on about how this new technology would transform my sales force and pay for itself repeatedly. Every time I tried to ask a question she offered another reason why Blackberry was the answer to all the world's troubles. Maybe I was partially responsible for her features monologue because I admitted during her first and only question that its features were of interest to me. Note to self: don't tell the truth to a sales rep ever again.

In her haste to share every detail about her product, she forgot to ask if I had the authority to spend tens of thousands of dollars for cutting-edge technology that would need to connect to our company servers. She just kept selling.

From where we were sitting in the conference room, I faced the windows into the main lobby. Every few minutes, one of my sales reps or a manager walked through the area, and I prayed that someone, anyone, would need me so I could escape from the Blackberry lady. Alas, they ignored me completely. Soon she was up to her fifteenth or fiftieth benefit. I can't quite remember which one.

"Did you know that a Blackberry has a full-size qwerty keyboard that will revolutionize how you send e-mail messages from your phone and sell more to more people?" she asked finally taking a breath. I realized then that she wasn't quite sure what we actually sold. Not being an extremely patient man back then (I am *so* much better now!), I eventually determined that only I could save myself from this pontificating predator. During her pause for a breath, I popped the question that salespeople often view as an invitation to close.

"How much will it cost to outfit my managers and sales team with Blackberrys?"

Although this question is not necessarily a sign that the prospect likes the product or an indication that the salesperson should begin pushing for a decision, many to most salespeople read it wrong and smell blood in the water. I could see the look of triumph in her eyes. She must have been thinking, *One or more of the features that I described have caught his attention and now I just need to massage the price discussion.*

She was wrong!

In my desperation to finish the meeting quickly, I had devised the perfect strategy to extricate myself from the situation in under ten minutes. Because she had never mentioned the price up to that point, and because I knew that the investment would be quite large, I had my out.

"Your cost per device excluding the monthly fees would be approximately five hundred dollars." Even a history major like me could figure out that she was describing a more than twenty-thousand-dollar investment.

I won!

She lost any chance for my business, and I could adjourn the meeting almost immediately.

"Oh, I am so sorry," I said, "but our budget won't allow for it this year. Could you follow up with me again in nine months before we create our new budgets?"

That stopped the meeting cold, and I made sure not to give her the name of my boss because I valued my position. I knew suggesting that one of my superiors meet with the Blackberry lady would have been a definite career killer.

The odd part of this experience was that my company could have benefited from Blackberry's technology. Approximately two years later we did move to the Blackberry platform and bought their phone for every manager and most reps. However, the lady who attempted to sell me on its features and benefits was no longer with the company. That didn't surprise me as she was insensitive to our needs and ultimately unable to close a big deal with a Fortune 500 company. I was a high-level Gatekeeper. Had she impressed me by understanding our process and our product, it might have opened doors for her to the next level of our company. Some of the top folks in information technology at our headquarters, no more than twenty miles up the road, were friends. I was also intrigued by the power that "smartphones" could bring to my sales professionals. With my advocacy, she could have moved further up into our company where someone might have made a decision to purchase her product. That is, I could have been of some assistance until I endured her features and benefits tirade.

DON'T BE THE BLACKBERRY LADY!

Think about a time in your life when you experienced something similar. I'm sure you feel my pain because everyone has dealt with a Blackberry lady multiple times in their lives. If you work in sales, you've likely built some immunity to the poor behavior of salespeople. Think of the cringe factor that you have experienced and triple that feeling—that's how your prospects feel.

While working on this chapter, I received a sales call on my cellphone. The pitch started out something like this:

"Hi, my name is Susie and I wanted to offer you a great vacation getaway. Because you have stayed with us before (she did not identify who, where, or when we stayed with her company) we wanted to offer you a great vacation in Orlando, Florida for 75 percent off our regular rate."

She didn't stop talking for approximately two minutes, because she was so excited to tell me "all the details of this trip." When she finally said that all I had to do was answer a few questions in order to receive five days in Orlando plus a two-day cruise plus "free breakfast, lunch, and dinner each day," I thanked her and hung up.

A BAD FIRST CALL

Let's examine standard practice for most salespeople in commoditized industries like insurance, office products, janitorial supplies, cellphones, automobiles, legal services, and technology. How would this line of questioning affect you if you were the prospect?

"Hi, my name is Tom from Tom's Commodity Solutions, and I would like to talk to the person who is responsible for buying my commodity. I have a price list that I would like to give them, and I am sure that if I saw all of your invoices I could prove that I am cheaper than whoever you use now."

This sales approach might be interpreted in the following manner by the prospect: "You're not important unless you are the person that deals with my commodity. You've made a stupid choice in suppliers. And only an idiot would pay as much as you do for the products you purchased."

Do you see the similarity between those two messages? I hope you do, because for those of you who wonder why reps can't grow their business, this could be the main reason. Prospects don't like to be called stupid and reps don't like rejection.

When have *you* been a prospect? Do you remember any specific incidents that made you sick to your stomach? Were you ever embarrassed from being manipulated or forced into purchasing a product you didn't want or need? Were you ever frustrated knowing that someone is wasting your precious time or shamed into feeling like a total dunce for buying from the salesperson's competitor? What feelings come to the surface?

A BETTER WAY TO APPROACH YOUR PROSPECT

Before we look at a better way to sell, consider some important facts about selling.

Two Sales Facts:
1. Most deals don't close on a first call.
2. Most salespeople don't act like number 1 is true.

One Prospect Fact:
1. Prospects dislike most salespeople because they ignore sales fact number 1.

Maybe the problem with the word *sales* is that it offers no differentiation between good and bad sales calls. Experiences like the Blackberry lady and the Orlando cruise lady should be called "verbal battery," rather than engaging with a prospect. No wonder prospects and customers detest most sales people. They are sick of being bludgeoned by sales pitches whose primary focus is exceeding call quotas, rather than becoming acquainted with a prospect and their company.

Hopefully, you have reconsidered what it feels like to be a prospect. So, what should it mean for you as a salesperson?

> A good first call can establish a positive relationship with the prospect and gives whoever establishes the relationship a positive feeling about it. . . When we try to accomplish everything at one time, we risk being perceived as pushy.

As I mentioned previously, part of the stress to close the sale comes from management's pressure to conform to call quotas. Close the sale and move on to the next prospect as quickly as possible.

How does that make the prospect feel?

Used. And for good reason!

But what if you tried a different approach? What if you made your first call to the prospect without any expectation of closing the sale?

It doesn't mean you'll win their business. However, a good first call can establish a positive relationship with the prospect and gives whoever establishes the relationship a positive feeling about it.

Does a first call need to accomplish more? I don't think so. When we try to accomplish everything at one time—get around the Gatekeeper, find the buyer, present our sales pitch (that they usually don't want), and ask for their business—we risk being perceived as obnoxious and pushy.

If you were in the prospect's shoes, wouldn't you feel that way about that sort of salesperson? We'll discuss a kinder approach for connecting with the prospect in chapter 4.

From my unofficial poll of sales reps, nine out of ten prospects respond to them with "We're happy with who we work with"—or something worse because they feel threatened, insulted, or they're actually sincere about their satisfaction with their current provider.

Change is hard for anyone to accept, much less embrace, unless there is an actual need not being met or pain that exists within a current relationship. Almost all sales training courses including Professional Selling Skills and Sandler Training use the terms *needs* or *pain* to describe how a prospect must feel before they will switch suppliers or add a new one.

They do such a good job of describing prospect's pain that I won't add much to their conclusions in this book.

However, there must be "pain" of some type in more than 10 percent of our prospects or our competitors are doing such a good job that we should find something else to sell. So, if we use a cold-calling process and the first call ends before it starts with 90 percent of our potential customers, we will fail miserably. Can any salesperson or team afford to be rejected by 80 or 90 out of 100 prospects and still grow their business? How much worse will it be when we inflict additional pain by insulting Gatekeepers or trying to manipulate another company's employees? If you were the prospect, wouldn't you become hardened to almost any sales pitch?

Smashing through myriads of prospects also ensures that the sales rep will push harder than he or she should with those who will meet with them. Do you see the trap? Is this type of sales process what you would want your company to be known for? The answer should be obvious.

Prospects, especially Gatekeepers, dislike salespeople because they often disrespect their time and ignore the Golden Rule: Do unto others as you would have them do unto you.

And, in my humble opinion, the biggest error of all for salespeople is to lead with price, like I illustrated above. There are multiple traps when a rep leads with price that can become catastrophic during the sales process—which I'll describe in the next chapter.

CHAPTER 3

THE PROBLEM WITH PRICE

"We Have The Lowest Prices Anywhere."
— Slogan on a vacant Ultimate Electronics store

If the company you sell for has the lowest possible prices in the marketplace, polish your resume. Either they will go out of business because they can't pay their overhead or their product or service is so unique they won't need salespeople to sell it for them.

Did you ever watch the TV show *The Office?* Most of the time the show made me cringe because it seemed like its episodes were inspired by companies for which I had worked or consulted. Truth be told, I was afraid to watch, because the situations were so bad and yet so realistic, it reminded me of someone scraping their fingernails on a chalkboard.

However, a few of their story lines intrigued me enough to tune in, even though at times I was tempted to run out of the room screaming. The most riveting episodes for me highlighted Michael's resignation from Dunder Mifflin to start his own company. The Michael Scott Paper Company added Pam and Ryan to its team, and they headquartered their startup in the broom closet in the basement of Dunder Mifflin's building.

In order to steal business from Dunder Mifflin quickly, they cut prices way below cost. Within a few weeks they gained a foothold in Scranton, while panic set in at Dunder Mifflin. Senior leadership from their former company visited to assess the situation. They were totally confounded by how Michael and his team could sell products so cheaply.

In the final episode, "Broke," Michael learned from his CPA that his start-up would be bankrupt in less than a month, because their prices were too low. At the same time the CFO of Dunder Mifflin decided to buy Michael's company because they had taken ten of the company's largest accounts. Only Dwight knew the truth about The Michael Scott Paper Company's financial situation, but no one would listen to him. Near the end of the final episode, Dunder Mifflin bought The Michael Scott Paper Company and rehired Michael, Pam, and Ryan—just as Michael was about to beg for his job back.

STOP THE PRICE-CUTTING INSANITY!

Price cutting can generate business temporarily, but at some point, companies and sales reps need to make a sustainable profit. Every sales organization emphasizes profitability within its ranks, but too many companies attempt to entice prospects with price-based ploys.

In their spectacular book *Blue Ocean Strategy*, Kim and Mauborgne describe the problem with the current competitive landscape. They point out that so many competitors occupy similar business spaces that commoditization of products and services has become rampant. In order to gain market share within commoditized industries, business leaders have emphasized price cutting and cost containment. Kim and Mauborgne call this sort of strategy competing in a red ocean.

Competing in red oceans can grow sales, but profits are continually threatened by other companies that perform the same functions at a lower cost. The book highlights the fact that many companies—and by extension salespeople—have fallen into the "lower price" trap only to be defeated by other, more efficient systems.

This scenario is being played out between numerous product-based companies that sell the same commodities as Amazon. If a company dares to compete with Amazon on price alone, it will lose. Amazon's cost structure is much lower than its competition, and Wall Street hasn't set the expectation that it needs to make money—yet. So, competing against Amazon without a strategy that deemphasizes price is competing in a vast red ocean that is doomed to fail.

The book suggests that companies must find ways to sail in Blue Oceans, where price competition is not the primary selling tool. The authors explain:

> What consistently separates winners from losers in creating blue oceans was their approach to strategy. The companies caught in the red ocean followed a conventional approach. . . . The creators of blue oceans, surprisingly, didn't use the competition as their benchmark. Instead they followed a different strategic logic that we call value innovation. Value innovation is the cornerstone of blue ocean strategy. We call it value innovation, because instead of focusing on beating the competition, you focus on making the competition irrelevant by creating a leap in value for buyers and your company, thereby opening new and uncontested market space. (W. Chan Kim and Renée Mauborgne, "Blue Ocean Strategy. Cambridge: Harvard Business Review Press, 2015, 12.)

Cirque du Soleil, Yellow Tail, and Southwest Airlines are examples the authors cite of companies that sail in blue oceans. Let's examine how Southwest Airlines has differentiated itself so well in the otherwise commoditized air travel environment.

HAPPY EMPLOYEES MEAN HAPPY CUSTOMERS

Southwest's mantra, "Bags Fly Free" has captured the hearts and minds of many regular travelers. As a frequent business traveler, I am extremely impressed by their creative advertising, efficient boarding process, and especially their workers. Their employees are motivated and empowered by management to do whatever it takes to serve the customer. Flight attendants often find ways to have fun with the rote safety warnings passengers must be subjected to on every flight, so they seem much more human.

Southwest is also smart enough to tell stories about exceptional acts of kindness performed by their employees in their monthly magazine. Bragging about an employee's kindness or personal sacrifice for a customer highlights the importance of their team and impresses their passengers. Not a bad way to build loyalty to their brand, right?

Please notice that we haven't said anything specific about their prices. However, in a recent nonscientific poll, all my friends with an opinion believed that Southwest Airlines is very low priced.

Again, because I travel almost every week and need to find reasonably priced flights, I can state without reservation that they are not always the cheapest. In fact, by the time you add the $15.00 fee that ensures an aisle or window seat, they are often more expensive than other carriers. But, no one seems to care about that fact. Southwest has done a great job of taking price pretty much out of the equation through their branding and marketing strategy.

But, do they make money? Over the past fifteen years they have been profitable more consistently than any US airline. They definitely sail in a Blue Ocean and have never gone bankrupt, while almost every other major airline serving North America has struggled to survive at one time or another.

THE RACE TO THE BOTTOM

Businesses must find ways to sail in blue oceans or risk failing. So, why do so many sales organizations struggle to differentiate themselves from the competition except through the use of price-based propositions? Moreover, why do the same companies feel the need to deceive current customers about price increases?

Yesterday I asked a business owner about the message his sales team uses to generate interest from their prospects. His answer mirrored the response from over 250 other owners I have spoken to in various fields.

"We try to get their attention by offering to save them money."

Then I asked him, "Can you actually save them much money on the products or services they purchase from you?"

"No," he replied. "We can't and that has always troubled me."

Price-based sales is a disease with many symptoms, but they almost always share the same outcomes:

1. Drastically shrinking profits
2. Diminishing commissions for reps
3. Increasing temptation to deceive prospects or customers
4. Companies acquiring their competitors because they can't grow organically

In the industry I am most familiar with, office products, the chickens have come home to roost for dealers that have focused strictly on price.

During a meeting with at least one thousand dealers and representatives, a wholesaler terrified the audience just by stating the number eight. According to a major study that they had just completed, the speaker explained that only 8 percent of the opportunities dealers generated—including request for quote, fax order forms with adjusted pricing, and unsolicited quotes—resulted in sustained new business.

Eight percent is a pathetic return on investment, especially considering the time and effort required to generate price quotes. The rep spends time, effort, and emotional energy obtaining the opportunity. Then either the rep or someone else in the office must create the customized quote that often takes multiple hours cross-referencing to ensure accuracy. Then, because the rep had not adequately differentiated him or herself from the competition, that quote could be handed back to the incumbent supplier who will then be asked to match or at least split the difference between their current pricing and the new offer.

The lack of response from so many prospects ensures that the reps will lose faith in their ability to gain new business through price-based or cold-calling techniques. This in turn lowers the acceptable margin for the company trying to acquire new business and leads to sales stagnation or even degradation.

Congratulations! If you participate in these types of drills in your industry, you are at least partially responsible for bringing down the market price or what I call leading the race to the bottom.

BREAK THE PRICE-CUTTING DEATH SPIRAL

So how do you get out of this horrible game? Your company must take at least four action steps to avoid this death spiral:

1. Stop trying to sell to every prospect.
2. Train your reps to ensure they are armed with the right questions to determine whether prospects might feel any pain besides price.
3. Determine if your competitors have issues that you can address (needs that you can

meet) or your product/service is actually a better fit for the prospect. If neither of these is true, don't waste their time or yours.

4. Give monetary rewards to any rep who finds a weakness besides price in one of your competitors.

Most managers know that yesterday is not like today and that selling tomorrow will be an adventure, no matter how prepared their salespeople are. They recognize the need to change their sales culture and in many cases, they are doing just that. However, I have observed far too many companies that compete in red oceans, feel burned by their investments in rep development, and are either maintaining their businesses or slowly dying.

Within the next few years they will need to either sell out or go away, because they cannot or will not change their sales culture. And there's one factor more than any other that prevents their sales culture from improving: the unchangeable sales rep.

As a general rule, the unchangeable rep is too focused on price, hates technology, most new ideas and being

> The key is to differentiate your company from the competition without resorting to price-based ploys. Establish excellent relationships and quickly determine if they are a possible fit for your company.

told anything about how to do their job more efficiently, effectively, or profitably. They love to talk about the good old days and how their customers need constant attention. Consequently, they claim they have no time to add new prospects or even penetrate more deeply into their current accounts. Ten years ago they might have been the top-performing rep in your company, but now they are in the middle of the pack or below. If you are a sales professional, could this be you? And even if they are still your best salesperson, is the company itself shrinking?

If these struggles seem at all familiar, there is hope. The rest of this book is designed to save companies and reps from themselves and their price-based styles. The changes could be painful to implement, but the success that a revitalized sales team brings to a company is worth the effort.

The key is to differentiate your company from the competition without resorting to price-based ploys. Beginning in the next chapter we will outline an approach to prospects that should enable you to establish an excellent relationship and quickly determine if they are a possible fit for your company. That doesn't mean the strategy will work in every case, but if your sales are slipping and your sales team will not change with the times, what have you got to lose?

CHAPTER 4

WHY YOU SHOULDN'T SELL _TO_ YOUR PROSPECT

Carl Jung once said, "The meeting of two personalities is like the contact of two chemical substances: if there is any reaction, both are transformed." That reminds me of when I was an awkward sophomore in high school just learning to relate to the opposite sex. I encountered a damsel in distress crying in the hallway. My family background taught me to be concerned about others and help them whenever possible. The fact that this girl was attractive only heightened my desire to be a friend in need.

We sat together on the hard tile floor, her tears a composite of anger and sadness, while she explained that her boyfriend had just broken up with her. "He ignores me at school, won't return my phone calls for days after I call him, and I just found out he's taking someone else to next week's dance."

And I listened.

"He broke every promise he ever made to me, and now he won't even look at me when we pass in the hall," she cried.

"Tell me about that," I said.

Every question I asked brought another wave of tears.

"He never really cared for me at all, and I have heard that he is making fun of me in front of anyone who will listen."

"Wow!" I replied. "What a jerk!"

"I know," she wailed. "I don't know why I put up with him."

I'd NEVER do that to you, I thought to myself.

And I didn't. By just trying to help someone in need, almost magically, a caring relationship developed. She eventually became my first girlfriend, due in large part to my listening skills, because I fulfilled a need of hers.

SELLING IS BUILDING RELATIONSHIPS

What do relationships have to do with selling products or services in the twenty-first century? Absolutely nothing on one level—yet in another sense it demonstrates the building blocks of value selling and customer relationships. Remember the old saw "Life is a sales job."

I guarantee that I was not the best-looking guy that young lady could have dated. I didn't letter in any sports. I was a fairly proficient snow skier, but there is no way she could have known that before we started going out. We began dating because I listened to the needs she expressed and showed compassion towards her circumstances. Could selling products and services be as easy as making a good impression on the prospect by being kind, trying to understand their needs, and providing well-positioned solutions?

Listening and caring builds relationships—and just to be clear, I never looked at dating as an opportunity to take advantage of a young woman. If your own history makes it hard to consider the similarities between selling and dating, I apologize. Manipulation should never be a part of any relationship.

Yet, prospects often believe that salespeople only want to take advantage of them. "Salespeople are only in it for the money," they complain. Or, "I can't trust anything a salesperson says because they always start pushing me to buy stuff I don't want."

Unfortunately, this is true in many cases. But it doesn't need to be this way, nor should it.

The relationships that a salesperson builds must be based upon unconditional positive regard, rather than serve as a means to an end. Let me illustrate this concept through another story from my high school experience.

I discovered girls in tenth grade. Compared to most guys my age, I started a little late, but I had an excuse. Actually, I had two excuses.

First, we had moved across the country to Colorado in the summer before ninth grade so when school started I didn't know anybody. Meeting friends of any gender was hard enough, so my ninth grade year was consumed with fitting in.

Second, I was a "dumb preacher's kid." Preacher's kids are known for causing trouble and being devious. Not me, especially when it came to girls. Except for my two sisters, I had hardly spent any time around girls growing up, and my father had only dated my mother before they married. I wasn't going to learn anything about girls from him.

So the first day of school in tenth grade I determined to find out how other guys became popular with girls. It didn't take long to discover one of their methods.

Standing in the school parking lot, I noticed a few guys leaning against their cars. They were laughing and once in a while one of them would shout something like, "Hey, baby! You look really good today. Where have you been all my life?" I also noticed that their catcalls only upset the young women. In return they either yelled something back at the guys about being jerks or sprinted toward the safety of the school door. Not one of those guys ever engaged any of those girls in a normal conversation. In fact, I don't remember any of them even being with a girl. I apologize if any of this description offends you. Trust me, it offended me as well. My parents taught me to treat everyone with respect. I determined that day that the parking-lot tactic was not for me.

On the contrary, I am convinced that a good salesperson selling a reputable product or service doesn't need to pressure anyone. They simply need to "date" their prospects. Pressuring the prospect to buy, changes the entire process in a very negative way.

GOOD SALESPEOPLE DON'T NEED TO BE PUSHY OR MANIPULATIVE

The 1970s band The Doors sang a song that highlights a sales approach that "reeks" of manipulation. "Hello, I Love You, Won't You Tell Me Your Name?"

The best salespeople avoid behavior that is manipulative because they don't like "being sold" any more than their prospects. No one does. So why can't sales organizations and reps just stop being pushy and manipulative?

Is it any wonder why so many Millennials hate sales people and prefer buying everything online? They crave relationships and good relationships take time to cultivate. However, many Baby Boomers and Gen Xers model sales behavior that ignores the personhood of their prospects. Even today, too many sales organizations trumpet that the value of their salespeople is directly tied to their ability to close. Could the high level of turnover within sales organizations be linked to the use of sales techniques that closely resemble the obnoxious guys I first observed in a high school parking lot?

I won over my first girlfriend because I listened to her pain and earned her trust not because of all my features, or because I was such a fine male specimen." Granted, sometimes especially attractive individuals can win people over very quickly due to their dynamic personality or stunning good looks. But, building a trusting relationship based only upon these traits can be perilous.

CONTINUOUS REJECTION CHANGES US FOR THE WORSE

Recently I spoke to a group of eight millennial salespeople. They were all astoundingly well spoken and attractive, the sort of individuals anyone would want to become acquainted with. So, I was fascinated by their cold-calling statistics.

"Using your sales process," I asked them, "how many cold calls do you need to make in order to set one appointment?" The answers were immediate and almost unanimous.

"We get rejected 9 out of 10 times in our territories," they responded, nearly in unison.

A few of the salespeople almost seemed gleeful as they answered. If I had been rejected 9 out of 10 times just to gain an appointment early in my sales career, I would have melted into a puddle on the floor.

Don't get me wrong. These young people are usually meeting their sales quotas, but what will happen if:

1. They run out of prospects within their territories and need to start over?
2. One or more of them lose their immunity to the rejection they experience day after day?
3. Or even worse, they become so callous about their prospects that they learn to completely ignore their feelings?

Have you ever met salespeople who seem to have lost all their concern for others? Getting to know them makes my skin crawl because they have only one focus: themselves. They don't care who they need to beat, debate, humiliate, or manipulate in order to get what they want— without the slightest concern as to how it affects others. To them, making lots of money crowds out every other motivation.

My sophomore year in college I worked as the assistant manager of a Soda Straw a now defunct regional chain of ice cream eateries. During the course of our business, I met a man I'll call "Jim." Jim was a car salesman (yes, car salespeople have _really_ impacted me!) who worked at the dealership across the street. He and his buddies came in almost everyday for lunch. While they talked shop, I listened.

"You should have seen how I financed the last sucker," one of them would say. "They won't be able to afford the payments, but I'll make great money on the commission." Then everyone would laugh and look to Jim for approval.

Jim had dark hair, wore nicely tailored suits, and ladies obviously found him very handsome. He was the best salesman at the car dealership. He exuded confidence and an aura I couldn't quite identify, at least at first. During the summer, Jim and I became better acquainted. He had been in car sales since high school and made tons of money. On more than one occasion he suggested that I had the right attributes to make a great salesman.

"Tom, you have a great smile, you resolve issues quickly, and you're a natural leader. You could make lots of money selling cars." While his compliments made me feel great about myself, I noticed that he never spoke of his prospects and customers in a positive way. They were "idiots" or "stupid," and he didn't even say anything positive about the salesmen whom he joined for lunch. But he told me he really liked me.

One day in the middle of the afternoon, he visited the restaurant by himself and asked for me to sit down with him, away from the handful of customers that were there at the time. "Tom, why don't you give up this college thing and join me across the street? Cars, women, money, that's what we all want, right? Well, I have them all, and if you work with me, it can all be yours."

The look on his face was simultaneously passionate and terrifying. I felt excitement, but even more, trepidation. "You're wasting your life," he told me. If I'd just follow him across the street, I could make a fortune. I felt like I was speaking with the devil incarnate.

I politely turned down his invitation because I sensed that success without morals would destroy me rather than complete me. Sales without any purpose except to win might enable me to be materially successful, but is that all life is about?

Obviously our families, friends, and acquaintances are important, but _every_ prospect and customer we sell to is important too. I worry for the young millennial salespeople I met because the many rejections they receive might beat them down over time. Even worse their negative sales experiences might cause them to value only results rather than the people who ultimately enable their success.

> Sales without morals will destroy you. There is more to life than closing the sale. Imagine how much more motivating it would be for those in your company if people were saying, "Thanks for coming by today."

My background, experience, and values have led me to create a different sales methodology. The techniques in this book have been specifically designed and tested to honor the value of the prospect as well as the salesperson. Both are valuable to their Creator and society, so doing anything to manipulate others in the pursuit of a sale must be exposed for what it is. Selling that is based only on self-gratification destroys the personhood of everyone involved.

Sales doesn't need to be reduced to something you don't like with people you don't know. Imagine how much more motivating it would be for those in your company if people were saying, "Thanks for coming by today."

In such a process, the company, the potential customer and the sales rep all win. In the next chapter we'll discuss how to initiate this process.

CHAPTER 5

ARE YOU A SOCIOPATH OR PSYCHOLOGIST?

"We get rejected on nine out of ten cold calls!"

I still cannot get that statement out of my head. Something is wrong with a process that accepts consistent rejection as a normal approach to sales. No wonder sales reps and prospects develop a resistance to each other that results in both groups treating each other like . . . well, like Republicans and Democrats.

Up to this point, I have attempted to show what is wrong with our current sales culture. For the rest of this book, I will describe an approach to sales that moves sales reps and prospects away from confrontation and towards collegiality.

COLD CALLING IS FOR SOCIOPATHS

I hope I haven't given you the impression that cold calling is easy. It is not.

Walking into an office with the intention of creating a relationship is tough; accomplishing the same goal over the telephone is even more difficult. I estimate that over 90 percent of people hate rejection—the rest are lying or are sociopaths.

Don't get me wrong, many businesses value sociopathic traits, like not taking no for an answer, because the sociopathic rep is more adept at pushing through a myriad of nos to get to a yes. However, in the previous four chapters I've shown how sociopathic behavior increases the probability that the prospect has needs the salesperson will never discover. Oftentimes the salesperson fails to make the sale not because the prospect has needs the salesperson can't meet, rather they have a distaste for the rep's persona.

Consider the last paragraph for a minute. Is it possible that you or your company are burning through too many prospects because your only goal is to find a decision maker that you can pitch your product to and close quickly?

What if slowing down the prospecting process by one or two calls ensured:

1.   Your rejection rate would fall from 9 out of 10 to 1 or 2 out of 10?
2.   You could successfully determine whether the prospect was the right candidate for your goods and/or services, rather than gauging the value of their account by whether or not they will quickly schedule a meeting?

3. Your approach would differentiate you from other sales people in a positive way?

THE BUXTON SCALE

In the 1980s and 90s I spent eight years in seminary obtaining a three-year master's degree. (Obviously, I wasn't a quick study.) While there we learned about the Engel Scale, which describes a person's progress toward a deeper faith in God on a scale of –13 to +13. However, it can be used to measure any sales process. For the sake of conversation, let's call this the Buxton Scale.

> Salespeople often fail to make the sale not because the prospect has needs the salesperson can't meet, rather they have a distaste for the person's sales pitch.

-13 -12 -11 -10 -9 -8 -7 -6 -5 -4 -3 -2 -1 0 1 2 3 4 5 6 7 8 9 10 11 12 13

Imagine that you are about to make a cold call to a prospect. Unless your company advertises heavily in social media and other expensive advertising mediums, your prospect likely knows nothing about your service or product, or you, and thus may be cold to your advances. Hence the term "cold call."

You might go to LinkedIn or sites like Searchbug.com to research the ultimate prospect, but often you will need to deal with a Gatekeeper who is taught to fend off cold callers. Again, if you haven't tried it, you have no idea how scary it is. Raise your hand if you really like rejection!

So on the Buxton Scale a −13 indicates that the prospect doesn't know who you are or what your company does. A +13 describes a customer who trusts you and your company so completely that they will follow any suggestion you make to them. The goal of this loyalty scale is to measure how strong your sales relationships are, but too many sales people forget this important fact. As a general rule, a positive sales relationship cannot be firmly established on one call. There must be a plan to move the prospect from not knowing you at all to establishing some trust. I guarantee you will experience results similar to these if you're willing to view the sales process in this way.

Because so many sales people forget that creating a sale takes time, the −13 describes where most cold calls start (whether in person or on the phone) and, most often within less than thirty seconds, end. In chapter 2 I suggested that selling the minute you walk through the door of a prospect or immediately when someone answers the phone can be disastrous. And yet, almost all salespeople begin their calls with this ridiculously canned mantra:

"Hi, my name is _____ from _____, and I would like to speak to the person who buys _____.

Where did everyone learn this?

The only problem with the Buxton Scale is that it doesn't indicate what happens after someone meets you and becomes even more negative about what you are selling. When you spend the first thirty seconds of every cold call explaining who you are and treating the Gatekeepers as if their importance is contingent on the role they play in buying your product, their anti-salesperson training immediately kicks in.

SHOW THE GATEKEEPER A LITTLE RESPECT!

Once you have interrupted the Gatekeeper and been rejected the first time, it is almost impossible to establish a relationship. As an example, how do you get past the Gatekeeper who says, "We're happy with our current supplier"? If you want to move more prospects from –13 to +1 or +2, you will need to revise your initial approach.

Here is what you should acknowledge before you speak to any Gatekeeper:

- They are important enough to the business that they have been given the responsibility of greeting customers and other guests. They are the face of the business.
- Everyone from the office manager to the highest ranking official in the company knows that person by name.
- From this we can infer that the Gatekeeper would probably be able to influence one of their superiors to visit with a salesperson— if they wanted to.

To confirm this, I have asked many CEOs, "Would you make an appointment to see someone based on the recommendation of your front office person?" In every case the answer was an enthusiastic "Yes!"

The Gatekeeper is the first line of defense against any intruders, especially solicitors. They have been tasked with guarding the time of the people in the office. The higher up the totem pole you go, the greater the responsibility of the Gatekeeper to guard that person's time.

MAKE A GREAT FIRST IMPRESSION

Here is a different way to use the first thirty seconds of your initial call.

When you walk into a prospect's office, do they know that you are a salesperson? Absolutely! Gatekeeper's can "smell" salespeople, so use that knowledge to your advantage.

Always dress for success. Men should wear a suit coats and possibly a tie if walking into a business office. In warm weather, you might get away with not wearing a coat but then a tie is mandatory. Women need to wear professional attire. Don't wear anything revealing or tight. If the prospect works on a job site and you are meeting in a construction trailer, dress in a professional yet practical manner.

Fortunately, Gatekeepers notice professional attire so much more now than they did in the past. Most salespeople reflect a business casual motif, which automatically differentiates those of us who dress more formally from those that believe in being "business casual."

A fascinating study called "The Traditional Communication Pie" suggests that 55 percent of the first impression you make during in-person meetings is based upon non-verbal factors including appearance, eye contact, posture, and facial expression. Another 38 percent of a prospect's first impression of you is determined by how you speak: your pitch, pace, volume, and emotion. The stunning statistic is that only 7 percent of a person's first impression of you is based upon the words you say.

Other studies suggest that first impressions are solidified in less than thirty seconds. Seven percent of a first impression is made by what you say, which means the relationship could be blown in less than seven seconds. Think about this. Prospects likely decide whether or not they like you within a few blinks of an eye. Given this, you should consider planning every first call before you enter the door.

Considering the fact that first impressions are so important, I prefer not to risk blowing my opportunity to develop a relationship with anyone by phone if possible. There are times where using a phone is the only medium available, so be aware that tone of voice and what you say become even more vital to your success. We will discuss cold calling on the phone in the FAQ section.

CREATING SUCCESS IN SEVEN SECONDS

Following the idea of dating the Gatekeeper, you need to think of each cold call as a first date. You are there to woo them by being sensitive to their needs. When I walk in the door I always wear a coat and tie. Also, whenever possible I partner with another salesperson.

Two professionals walking into an office immediately draw the Gatekeeper's attention. I always use that to my advantage. Whenever I walk through the prospect's door and see the Gatekeeper for the first time, I often say, "Yes, it's a couple of salespeople. Is it the smell?" This hokey phrase breaks the ice almost every time. You can come up with your own ice-breaker if you don't like mine, but it's important to have some tool for reducing the tension. If the person at the front desk relaxes his or her shoulders just a bit or smiles, you have won the seven second battle referred to above. Generally, they will allow you an opportunity to introduce the reason for your call as long as it doesn't take too much of their time.

Then comes the hard part. How do you avoid sounding "sales-y" while still giving the Gatekeeper some idea of the purpose for your visit?

"My name is Tom, and I'll bet you have a great [widget provider, service provider]." This simple sentence adds credibility, while taking away their favorite method of banishing sales reps. The Gatekeeper can't use the phrase, "We are very happy with our current supplier." You just assured them that you know they're happy. Furthermore the Gatekeeper immediately knows that you aren't pitching necklaces or religion. By mentioning your service or product category, you will elevate their interest to some degree, as long as you haven't interrupted them during an extremely stressful moment. (See the FAQ section on page 129 for a discussion of how to handle extremely busy Gatekeepers and No Soliciting signs.)

I can nearly guarantee that by using this approach, the Gatekeeper will become intrigued enough with your style to give you another twenty seconds or so to complete your call.

The second reason I always take a partner with me on a sales call is so while one of you is taking the lead the other can observe important facts about the office. If your company sells products, they can be looking for items from your competition. If your company sells information technology or a service, he/she can attempt to evaluate the company's, values, or priorities. Just seeing the layout of the office can provide hints as to the hierarchy, culture and openness a company has to change. Wide open floorplans with multiple sets of low cubicals can indicate openness to innovation, while a totally isolated reception area might suggest an adherence to tradition. Pictures, newspaper clippings, and even the type of reading material available for guests or its absence might provide some clues to whether this company will be a good prospect. Some of these insights can be gained from visiting their website, but there is no replacement for personally observing a company's culture.

DON'T SELL ON YOUR FIRST CALL

"But, Tom," you might say. "No one can describe their products or services in twenty seconds." Correct, you won't be able to sell them on your product or service or even attempt to get around them in twenty seconds.

If you initiate a normal sales call during the extra few seconds that the Gatekeeper rewards you for approaching them in an unusual manner, they will recognize their mistake quickly. Their renewed conviction that you are just like every other rep they have encountered in the past will ensure that your efforts will go down in flames at least nine out of ten times.

Alternatively, if you determine not to sell anything but rather you desire just to meet the Gatekeeper, your chances of being rejected will almost disappear.

My initial call to the Gatekeeper at any size company goes something like this:

"Yes, we're a couple of sales reps, do we smell like it?" (For details about where to stand and how to move closer to the Gatekeeper, see the FAQ section on page 129.)

"Yes, I guessed you were salespeople."

"My name is Tom and this is Sophie. I bet you have a great software provider."

"Yes, we do. We are very happy."

"Most people are happy with their vendors. May I ask you a question?" (At this point, the Gatekeeper will feel the call turning into some sort of sales pitch.)

"Do you like free purple pens? I happen to have one with me."

"Yes, I love free pens, especially purple."

"Great. Here it is. My name is Tom. Yours is—?"

"My name is Evelyn."

"Thank you, Evelyn. And believe it or not that is all we wanted to do today. We just wanted to meet you, because there are so many pushy salespeople out there that we wanted to become acquainted in a less intimidating way. Could I get a card from you please?"

At this point, the Gatekeeper will often guide you to the card of the person who is responsible for that commodity. But don't jump at the opportunity. You are there to meet the Gatekeeper and even if she offers to find the buyer, don't risk it. Interrupting the Gatekeeper's day is perilous enough. Assuming that the buyer would actually like to meet you at that moment is like betting on an inside straight in poker.

It doesn't usually work and could destroy any chance of moving toward a meeting. My recommendation is if the Gatekeeper offers to have you meet the buyer, thank her for the invitation, but decline. Then ask the Gatekeeper if you can provide a free pen for the buyer as well.

"Evelyn, would it be okay for Sophie or me to stop back the next time we're in the area and have something

to share with you that might be of value for your
company?"

"That would be fine."

YOUR GOAL IS TO BUILD RELATIONSHIPS

This corny approach works for me over 90 percent
of the time. But, I can hear you say, "What did this call
accomplish? You didn't ask for the name of the buyer
nor did you set up a firm appointment. Also, Evelyn
doesn't even know which company you're with, so how
could she contact you if she wanted to? How can you sell
when you don't say a thing about your product, service or
company?"

Ah! In my opinion, that is the key point. We began a
relationship not based on a product, service, or a company.
This technique is powerful if you actually want to create
relationships, so we accomplished a significant amount.
First, we weren't told that we weren't welcome in the office;
in fact we received permission to come back. Second, we
didn't try to get around the Gatekeeper or wow her with
super low prices or offers. Not to mention the fact that
relationship-oriented sales reps wouldn't feel the need to
move so far out of their comfort zone when using this
technique. This cuts down on the expense of regularly
replacing reps. If the Gatekeeper has allowed you to have
a short period of time to speak with them, what should
you attempt to accomplish? Since you won't close a sale in
twenty seconds, use the time to make a good impression.

Because I often teach salespeople in the office products industry, I use my extra twenty seconds to provide the Gatekeeper with a purple pen. Obviously, you could provide a gift that is more appropriate in your industry, but you could do worse than trying the purple pen approach. Why? In the hundreds of cold calls I have made I have found purple pens to be popular with almost everyone. Over 95 percent of the women, and most of the men, to whom I have offered a purple pen have been anywhere from excited to ecstatic to receive one. (See the FAQ section on page 129 for information on how to successfully give purple pens to men.) Purple is not a color that most companies use. Also, pens are among the most emotional items used in an office. If you don't believe me, ask everyone to hold up their pen at the next group meeting you attend.

Giving a purple pen to the Gatekeeper and not trying to sell them on anything that day has enabled every sales force that has attempted it to minimize rejection immediately. It also moves the prospect up the relationship scale from −13 to maybe −6. This doesn't mean that they will end up buying from your company, but it *will* enable the sales professional to bond to some degree with the Gatekeeper.

In the next chapter we will discuss how to quickly follow up with the Gatekeeper and move them further up the loyalty scale. Successfully completing the steps outlined in chapter 6 will strengthen the relationship with the

Gatekeeper. It also significantly improves the possibility of meeting with the appropriate decision makers within many more prospects than could be accomplished using sociopathic techniques.

CHAPTER 6

THE SECOND CALL: MOVING TOWARDS A MEETING

You left the office without leaving a business card, without even saying what company you work for, and without getting the name of the buyer. All you did was greet the Gatekeeper and give them a purple pen.

"What just happened?" the Gatekeeper will remark to someone in the office the moment you leave. "I think that was a sales call, but it's not like anything I have ever experienced. They were trying to sell something, right? And where were they from anyway?"

Don't worry, a mystery can be interesting, especially when the subject is sales. On many occasions, I have observed the Gatekeeper or Gatekeepers discuss our unexpected interaction as I walked out of the office—and their reaction has always been fascinating.

"WAIT," you might be yelling (with your inside voice, of course!). "I FORGOT TO LEAVE MY CARD. HOW WILL THE GATEKEEPER KNOW WHO I AM?"

To be fair, some Gatekeepers will ask who you're with, so always bring a business card—but don't offer it unless they ask. I never mention the name of my company in the initial call because there is a better way to introduce your company. Much better.

Also, because most salespeople begin each call by talking about their company, *not* providing a card differentiates you even more from them. Don't worry, though. If you follow the steps listed below, prospects will actually like the way you introduce them to your company.

> Because most salespeople begin each call by talking about their company, not providing a card differentiates you even more from them.

SEND A HANDWRITTEN NOTE

Assuming that you have a business card from the prospective company along with the Gatekeeper's name, you are set for the next step. However, after your first visit you might decide that the business doesn't fit your criteria. It didn't seem big enough or the Gatekeeper indicated that they don't use your product. If that is true, you don't need to carry on with the process which enables you to focus on prospects who have potential.

If the prospect looks promising, move to the next step of dating the Gatekeeper. On the same day you make the cold call, send the person a handwritten thank-you note with your business card in it. Send it via "snail mail," *never* as an e-mail.

The card should say something like:

Thank you for being so kind to me during our visit today. We know that you must be very busy, so be assured that I will do my best to never overstay my welcome. Sophie and I look forward to meeting you sometime next week to drop off some information that might be of value to your company.

Thanks again,

Tom & Sophie

A thank-you note is important because the few minutes it takes to send personalized handwritten comments to the Gatekeeper will further help you to stand out from other reps. It is also important to send the note on the same day you make the call because being a salesperson, you can get overwhelmed with work. Sending the note the same day ensures you remember and makes further progress with the Gatekeeper.

Writing a thank you note only takes a few minutes, but creating personalized comments that the Gatekeeper can relate to will take enough effort to limit the number of notes that most reps will want to create each day. Also, it is very important to not allow oneself to postpone this process, because procrastination leads to wasting the opportunity to move forward after completing the most uncomfortable single event in the entire sales process.

In my experience, sales blitzes where sales professionals make cold calls for half the day or all day don't work. Regardless of the number of new prospects they identify, most salespeople lack the time or organizational prowess to properly follow up on all of them. So, even good prospects might not receive a follow-up communication for weeks or even months.

Also, because of the penchant for salespeople to be a bit disorganized, the chances of placing forty leads in a customer relationship management (CRM) tool in a timely fashion are minimal. The rock band Chicago provided the best direction on how to be organized, although it definitely wasn't their intention.

The subject of their song "25 or 6 to 4" involved nothing more than the writer waking up at 25 or 26 to 4 am. I was very disappointed when I found out how inconsequential it was. However, I use it as a mnemonic device to organize my CRM.

- **25** excellent prospects with dates to follow up, ruthlessly evaluated for their potential.
- **6** or more meetings will come from those 25 prospects.
- **4** to 6 prospects should become customers if our product/service addresses their needs.

This translates to a 25 percent close rate—and my experience suggests that the real closing percentage is probably even higher. However, one behavior almost always kills the process in its tracks: moving from building a relationship to selling too quickly. This obliterates any progress a salesperson makes. Gatekeepers and buyers know that salespeople make their living through selling, so don't spend your hard-won credibility stating the obvious. Add value and avoid "sales-ish" techniques, at least through the third call.

SET UP AN APPOINTMENT AND LISTEN TO *THEIR* NEEDS

The goal of the second call is to set up an appointment with the Gatekeeper and whoever they recommend. It is also intended to help the salesperson understand more about the company's needs. This call is the most difficult to perform effectively and may be necessary to repeat a few times with the same prospect in order to be successful.

I can hear many of you saying, "This process is going to take forever if I'm forced to date the Gatekeeper. They probably have no background to discuss the product/ service I want to sell, so why do I need to include them?" Now calm down. There is a reason for this. If you ask to set up a meeting with them toward the end of the second call and they believe that you honestly care about the relationship you began through the cold call and handwritten note, then suggesting to the Gatekeeper that you would like to set up an appointment to meet them *and* whoever else they recommend often opens the door to the sale. Also you should affirm the Gatekeeper because all people are important in their own right. Manipulating your relationship with them just to meet the decision maker will slowly twist your entire being. Don't strive to be like the sales guy I met while working at the Soda Straw.

If you move the Gatekeeper from −13 to −3 or −4 by differentiating your sales process from others, they will feel more relaxed about telling you what involvement, if any, they have with the product or service you sell. A person like the Gatekeeper who remains friendly during the process is worth some investment on the salesperson's part.

Often the Gatekeeper will say, "I have nothing to do with making those decisions, but Sheri does." Obviously, this is a very positive development in the attempt to gain this company's business, so let's walk through how to get there on the second call.

NOW IT'S TIME TO MAKE YOUR VISIT

Approximately one week and not more than ten days after the cold call, visit your prospect again. This ensures they have received your thank-you note in the mail, and it should guarantee that they have not forgotten the original call.

Before you go make up a flyer to give the Gatekeeper. Don't include prices or even a sales offer. Rather, make sure the flyer provides the Gatekeeper and her buyer with valuable insight into whatever your company sells. They could include tips about improving heating and cooling efficiency, testing computers for malware, effective ways to minimize sickness in the office, or how to ensure that office chairs last longer. The tips on the flyer add value without creating sales tension.

When you enter the office, greet the Gatekeeper by name as you walk in the door and ask how their week has been. If two Gatekeepers are present, be sure to greet them both by name. Always restate that you heard them when they said they were happy with their current supplier. Then hand them the flyer and say something like, "I am thrilled when my customers are loyal, so if it's alright, I'd like to leave you with some solutions to common issues with our type of product. You'll notice that they don't include prices or specific sales offers so maybe you will want to ask your current provider for help with these ideas."

Wait? What did I just suggest? It's true, I mentioned that they might want to enlist their current supplier (boyfriend) to assist them. If you agree with my contention that everyone has some sort of relationship with the company (and sales rep or process) from which they buy a product or service, why not acknowledge it?

Such a recommendation demonstrates the Millionaire Mindset that Sandler Sales Training introduced years ago. It asks the question, "If you had a million dollars in your back pocket, would you sell differently?" If I had a million dollars in my pocket and still *wanted* to work in sales, I would sell differently. Wouldn't you? We wouldn't have the stress of needing to hit sales numbers to pay our bills or wondering if this particular call was going to be a waste. If I am a millionaire, my whole attitude towards sales changes, and it is very refreshing for the prospects that I meet.

If I don't have your business but I'm willing to help your company without any promise of future sales, I am again differentiating myself from other suppliers the Gatekeeper has encountered. If you provide enough assistance, quite often the Gatekeeper will actually ask, "But, couldn't you provide that for us?"

My answer has always been, "Of course I could be of assistance, but I want to respect your current relationship." This sort of interaction doesn't occur that often, but any act of kindness that differentiates you from your competition is always worth the effort.

DON'T FORGET THAT BREAKING UP IS HARD TO DO!

Remember that every company has a "boyfriend" or "girlfriend" for every product they buy, whether it is a virtual relationship or a real person. Have you considered that everyone in sales is, to some degree, a homewrecker because they are trying to uproot and replace a current relationship? So, do you really want to upstage or disparage a current boyfriend or girlfriend on the first, second, or any call?

All too often sales people experience rejection because they forget they are insulting the person they are trying to impress by attacking the decisions that have been made in the past. So, whatever you do, focus on adding value, not demonstrating weaknesses in your competitor's program.

The toughest part of the second call occurs after you provide the Gatekeeper with valuable advice or information. It's time to ask for a meeting. Say something like:

Is there a time I could set up an appointment with you and whoever you recommend, so I can understand more about your company? Whether you decide to use our services or not, I would love to understand more about how you choose vendors and what your company plans are in the coming months. It would also help me to become better informed about your values and processes so I can be of more assistance to my customers.

This question approach is different than the manner in which most sales people ask for the appointment. Does the following phrase sound familiar to you? "Could I meet with you so I can tell you about Tom's Commodity Company?"

If you have made a positive impression, the Gatekeeper will tell you at this moment whether they have any involvement in the decision-making process for the commodity you sell and the name of the correct person to talk to.

This may also occur during the first call without your even asking. But if the Gatekeeper reveals the person's name after you asked the question above during the second visit it tells you that you have moved even further up the loyalty scale. An actual relationship with the Gatekeeper could be emerging.

FOCUS ON THE PROSPECT

At least nine out of ten times, we're wrong to assume that prospects are interested in hearing about what we do or why our company is better. Even when we successfully schedule an appointment with that tenth company, most will quickly lose interest in the meeting if we make it all about our company and product or service. And yet, most of the sales people I have encountered, both as a manager and as a prospect, "show up and throw up."

To argue this another way, do people like talking about themselves or listening to others? We'll discuss this concept more in the next chapter, but for now, evaluate how much talking you do when you meet with the Gatekeeper.

At the end of the second call, asking for a meeting is a pivotal moment in the relationship.

The Gatekeeper could respond positively to your request for a meeting during the second call. At that point, they might become your coach within the company unless she is the decision maker, in which case you will be glad you didn't try to get around her. This exact scenario happened just a few weeks ago for a young woman who attended one of my seminars. She set up a meeting with her first two prospects using this technique.

However, a negative response from the Gatekeeper doesn't necessarily mean an end to the opportunity. Obviously, we hope they say yes to our request and set up a meeting with the decision maker. If our approach has been non-threatening, the relationship we began to build with the Gatekeeper through the first call, thank-you note, and second call, might survive.

Again, our fate lies in the hands of the Gatekeeper, and we need to listen carefully to their response. If they say, "I am not in charge of purchasing the commodity you are selling and Sarah is too busy to see anyone at this time," be sure to thank her for letting you know. Ask for permission to continue providing them with materials that benefit their company and if you can leave a gift for Sarah like the one you gave the Gatekeeper during the first call. You might even ask the Gatekeeper if you could connect with them on LinkedIn. Generally, they'll say yes to your requests, but even if the Gatekeeper states that he prefers you didn't call on them regularly, a positive connection might now exist.

AFTER THE DATE, EVALUATE!

Once you leave the office, determine how to list this prospect in your CRM. Calling on them again in one to six months, while sending Sarah and the Gatekeeper a few targeted emails in-between, can keep the relationship alive. This prospect might not be one of your top twenty-five, but leaving yourself notes in the calendar to regularly connect with them couldn't hurt.

Of course, other possibilities exist. The Gatekeeper could tell you that they can't meet at the present time but they are open to continued visits. If this happens, create a set of marketing pieces that provide solutions, not price-based enticements, that you can leave with them. After a few of these types of calls, the Gatekeeper may decide that you are giving her company more attention than her current boyfriend and change her mind about meeting with you.

Once the appointment is set, the real fun begins. We will discuss meeting preparation and reasonable goals in the next chapter.

CHAPTER 7

YOU SCHEDULED
A MEETING—NOW WHAT?

"We will send a technician to evaluate your roof and determine your needs. With our company, you will never need to deal with a salesperson."
—Radio advertisement for a roofing company

Our culture often suggests that meeting with a salesperson should be avoided at all costs. Thus far, we have outlined some of the reasons behind society's aversion to us, but hearing companies differentiate themselves by disparaging the entire profession still bothers me.

However, we can learn something from this roofing company's message. Prospects want to buy from someone who understands their needs and won't take advantage of them. To be good at sales we must be knowledgeable like a technician and evaluate the prospect's needs like a consultant. Never forget these axioms when you prepare for a meeting with a prospect or customer.

Prospects want to buy from someone who understands their needs and won't take advantage of them.

DON'T BE LIKE THIS SALESPERSON!

A few days ago, as I was contemplating the task of writing this chapter and whether it would be valuable to provide basic meeting information, I attended an event that reminded me why we must always review our sales process. The presenter started the sales call by saying, "We provide the very best solution for your company's challenges, and I will use a few examples to demonstrate my point." I spent the next hour in a sales torture chamber.

No introduction! No consideration was given to the fact that the attendees might have some concepts that they might want to explore. In fact, the salesperson didn't ask any questions during our hour together and made us feel like we were interrupting whenever we attempted to ask for clarification. "Pardon me, what is your process for determining whether our company is a good candidate for your product?" When I asked this question the salesperson looked at me like I was interrupting an important feature.

He said, "I think our proposal will answer that question more than adequately." With that he went on with his diatribe. Twenty-five minutes into the call—and before he even gave us an opportunity to ask about the overall cost—he explained:

> Maybe you have some concerns about whether the money you will need to invest in this project will gain you a significant profit. Let me tell you about the ABC company. They had the same concern and we made them millions. All you need to do is trust our experience in this area. It probably sounds like a very large investment, but you will see a return very quickly. We will even give some of your money back if you aren't completely satisfied with our performance. In fact, I know that I can get my boss to sign off on a larger than normal refund if you're dissatisfied, but I know that won't happen.

The salesperson had met only one of the three people in our group, but he assumed he knew all of our needs. Before asking us any questions, he had determined that the goal of our meeting was for him to explain the features they offered, which would definitely benefit us if we were smart enough to realize it. To us, the features/benefits strategy he employed proved that closing the sale was his only goal and nothing we said or *tried* to ask would get in the way. By the end of the meeting all three of us wanted nothing to do with the salesperson or his company, even though we definitely needed assistance with the commodity he was pitching.

Don't be like the salesman I just described. Plan every call ahead of time and use every tool possible to understand and connect with your prospect. You will be much more successful when *they* buy, rather than when *you* sell.

THE FIRST FIVE MINUTES WILL MAKE OR BREAK THE MEETING

Unless you sell a product that is in universal demand, research the company on the Internet to understand how your offering could help them. Look at the company's LinkedIn and Facebook pages as well as the their website. Also database clearinghouse company Zoominfo.com can provide a treasure trove of helpful information. If you determine that your prospect doesn't need your product or service, be sure to contact them in advance to clarify your findings. Never waste your time or theirs on a meeting that won't add value for the prospect.

Your first five minutes will almost always set the tone. So don't blow it! Greet the Gatekeeper warmly whether the person will be in the meeting or not. You couldn't have made it to this point without them, so always go out of your way to be gracious.

The Professional Selling Skills (PSS) program, offered by the Sales Alliance (sales-alliance.com), Sandler Training (sandler.com), and other organizations, offer excellent resources that ensure your meeting starts well. I will highlight a few of their better ideas here and let you research the introductory steps more thoroughly.

Too often salespeople will start a call without any structured plan. Many salespeople believe that following a plan to begin the meeting is too stifling, preferring to "go with the flow." In my experience, salespeople who lack a disciplined approach to engaging the prospect during the opening more often fail to win the business than those who follow a plan.

A common sales ploy is to look at pictures or memorabilia in the person's office and comment on them. Or, if the meeting takes place in a conference room, many reps spend time admiring a picture or decoration on the way through the office. Don't do that—unless the prospect makes a comment about it.

Sandler suggests that there must be four distinct parts to the opening of a call. The following is Sandler's plan for opening any sales call (after an appropriate amount of small talk). When it comes to small talk, follow the prospect's lead. If they want to discuss the weather or sports, feel free to join in, but do not try to top their story. Move towards the meeting introduction within a few minutes at the most. Respect the schedule that you have set with them and never go over the allotted time without prior permission from the prospect.

Step 1. Thank the prospect for setting up the meeting with you.
Step 2. Confirm the amount of time allowed for the meeting. I like to ask for thirty to forty-five minutes.
Step 3. State the purpose of the call. Practice a statement like, "Today, I was hoping that I could

learn more about your company along with its
focus and priorities, so you can determine whether
our services/product might be worth considering."
**Step 4 Check for acceptance by asking "Is
that ok with you?"** This is the most important
and least intuitive of the four steps to open the
call. If the prospect accepts your summary of the
purpose, they are confirming that they have an
interest and possibly a need for the product or
service your company offers. More important,
by asking them to confirm the content of the
call, you have put them in charge of its direction
and timing. Everyone wants to feel like they
are in control, especially when meeting with
salespeople.

BEGIN BY PROBING YOUR PROSPECT

The next step in a call can be remembered easily
using PSS's term, "Probing". The term perfectly describes
the care required to adequately understand the prospect's
needs. In most cases, the Gatekeeper or the buyer wouldn't
have scheduled a meeting with you if they didn't believe
they could improve their current process.

As I mentioned in the last chapter, the absolute worst
thing you can do is begin any call by talking about your
company. The prospect won't care about your company's
products or services if they don't meet their needs. The
temptation to jump right in and sell your company is so

pervasive and damaging to a possible sales relationship that it should never be employed.

Bragging about your company before you know the prospect's needs is like throwing "stuff" against a wall and hoping something sticks. In most cases, all you have left is a smelly mess that destroys any chance for moving the prospect further up the loyalty scale. However, be prepared with a quick summary statement about your company and the types of issues that you solve.

The challenge and excitement of sales involves asking the right questions that will help you understand *their* company, *their* culture, and to discover areas where they might be dissatisfied with their current "boyfriend." Even if you are selling a completely new product or service, understanding more about their company will provide you with vital information to help you determine whether their needs match your company's offering.

The following are a few questions that will help *you* understand the prospect better and help *them* discover possible needs. The questions focus on broad aspects and narrow as they progress. Don't ask closed-ended (yes and no) questions. Instead make it a point to use what Match.com claims to be the single most important phrase to expand any relationship: "Tell me about that" (TMAT).

1. "I reviewed your website, but I'm not sure I understand the total scope of what you do. Would you mind taking a few minutes to describe your goals

for this year and the [fact they may have highlighted on their website]?" Then include some follow-up questions: "How is that working out? How does it fit in with your overall goals?"

2. "Would you mind telling me the three criteria your company uses to choose vendors and if anything has changed within that process during the past year?"

They will probably share that they choose vendors based on price and service. This is a standard response that they learn in Purchasing 101. They might struggle with finding a third reason for choosing vendors, but that reason could be the key to unlocking existing pain if there is any. So be prepared with a response that they are not accustomed to hearing. In your initial cold call you suggested that they were probably happy with their current supplier, so "double-down" on that thought by asking a third question.

3. "Could we talk about the first reason you mentioned for a moment? What percentage of your decision-making about vendors is based on them maintaining the lowest price? The reason I asked the question is because we are competitive, but I know that we cannot provide the lowest prices available on all of the products/ services we sell. In fact, I'm not sure who can."

They may stammer for a minute, because almost everyone tries to avoid talking about price until the last possible moment. But by attacking it head-on you are finding out if the prospect is viable. If the buyer or Gatekeeper re-emphasizes that they always buy on the basis of the cheapest price, they have just disqualified themselves from enjoying your services. You can celebrate the fact that you will not need to waste your time chasing their business, because one way or another the effort will result in a race to the bottom between you and their current boyfriend. In that sort of circumstance, I'm betting on the boyfriend.

However, most prospects will answer the question about who has the lowest price by agreeing that nobody can always have the lowest price on all products or services. This enables you to focus on finding the best fit for the prospect and it raises your credibility to a much higher level. When you are completely honest and up front, most people want to find a way to buy from you.

Before every call I remind myself, *"The person who brings up price last loses."*

4. "How do you define and measure good service?"

This question will start the process of finding "pain" as Sandler Sales Training and many others call it or the "need behind the need" in PSS. The buyer scheduled the meeting because they feel some sort of pain or want to determine if they are missing something that will help their company become more efficient. Now we get to play detectives and discover what motivates the prospect.

Obviously, if they act like they want to move the meeting along more quickly (i.e. looking at the clock or their cell phones), just ask them how they would like it to proceed. However, if they seem to enjoy talking about their company or their process, let them do it.

5. "What other issues besides price and service influence your decision to change suppliers?"

You should be in no hurry as long as there is an adequate amount of time allotted for the meeting. Remember that the two of you are dating, and if you listen well, their number on the Buxton scale will continue to rise, ultimately resulting in a buying relationship.

Notice that I'm not suggesting you make much of an effort to discuss your product or service up to this point in the meeting. The prospect will move you toward that point if they appreciate the manner in which you sought to understand them and their company. In general, prospects are quite pleased when you avoid confronting them with a sales pitch within the first few minutes. They may direct the call to your product/service very quickly or spend time describing the inner workings of their company. Do you see the importance of opening the call with a check for acceptance? Follow their lead. Again, they know that you asked for the meeting with the intention of selling something.

If the flow of the call is handed to you, thoroughly review the prospect's perception of their business, their criteria concerning vendors, and their challenges (if they have any). At that time, questions about your specific product or service will be much better received. (Up to this point, the entire call should have taken somewhere between fifteen and twenty-five minutes.)

Properly connecting with the buyer should ensure that the call can go longer than scheduled if necessary, but be sure to confirm it with the participants at least fifteen minutes prior to the agreed upon ending time. (In the Frequently Asked Questions section on page 129 we discuss the process of managing a call when the prospect can only meet for fifteen minutes or less.)

> Properly connecting with the buyer should ensure that the call can go longer than scheduled if necessary.

NOW YOU CAN DEVELOP OPPORTUNITIES

Properly executing the next portion of the initial meeting depends on whether the product or service you are selling is revolutionary or if your product or service is meant to replace that of their current boyfriend.

If your product is exceptionally different from your competitors, ask for permission to describe it and how it has improved other companies' efficiency. Be sure to ask questions often to ensure that you aren't performing a monologue in front of a trapped audience. Ask them if the

service or product you have described might be beneficial
to them and if so, how? If they acknowledge that there
might be some value depending on the price and how
hard it would be to implement, you are ready to move on
toward summarizing, presenting, reversing, and next steps
which we will discuss in chapter 8.

A similar process of questioning works well
when your goal is to supplant their current boyfriend.
However, the questions must be much more targeted
toward your company's strengths when compared to
the competition. This is where it is beneficial to know
who your prospect is dating, but many buyers take
offense at being asked directly about their boyfriend.
Consequently, don't ask the Gatekeeper or the buyer about
the identity of their boyfriend. This directly conflicts
with the practices of many sales organizations, so you
will need to decide how to proceed. If your company's
strengths are exceptional compared to the competition,
carefully consider whether trying to discover the identity
of the boyfriend is worth the risk of offending the
prospect.

During the two visits before the initial meeting,
I always make it a priority to gather data through
observation, reviewing their website, or in some cases
gaining information from their sales force. (If your
prospect is a business, connecting with a member of their
sales team can be a goldmine of information for you
and them.) However, if you have researched all possible

avenues without success and need the information in order to proceed, do it carefully. If you must ask, say something positive or at least nothing negative about their boyfriend Think about it; how would you like someone telling you that your significant other is really ugly?

Notice that I have taken a significant amount of space discussing dangers within the questioning process without directly discussing how to find and extenuate pain. What good does it do to find the pain if you've already ticked off your prospect?

So if you avoid all the possible traps that salespeople often fall into, the prospect's pain should be easy to find. That is, if they have any pain and they perceive that you are different from other salespeople, chances are they will share it with you. If they didn't share anything when you asked how they defined good service, ask them about the products or services they use now. What do they like about the product or service and what do they wish could be improved.

If you sell insurance, they may be concerned whether their coverages are adequate and would appreciate an outside party validating it for them. If you sell copiers, they may question how long a service call should take to complete. In office products, billing issues can often be a challenge.

Prospect pain can take many forms, but if it is important to them, it should be important to you. Reflect back to the customer any statement that they make about their pain in order to be sure you understand it. Remember to add a TMAT to improve your understanding of the challenge and to ensure you understand their feelings on the issue.

In order to have a chance at supplanting the old "flame," at least two or three separate major problem areas must be evident. Do not attempt to address each issue as they divulge it with the old "feature and benefit" sales job. Moving the prospect toward the final stages (–2 or –1) before they become a customer often involves a realization on their part that you understand them better than their current "significant other." Listening attentively and refusing to interrupt their thoughts by suggesting solutions will set you apart from most of the competition. Be sure you don't rush to solve their issues (sell) until you understand them thoroughly. Only after they have adequately shared all their pain will they be ready to move toward any suggested solutions.

We will explore how to discuss possible solutions for their pain and how to create a positive conclusion to any call in the next chapter. We will also tackle the question, "What if the prospect doesn't have any pain?"

CHAPTER 8

"WOULD YOU
JUST LISTEN PLEASE?"

Famous Indian nonviolent freedom fighter Mahatma Gandhi once said, "Earth provides enough to satisfy every man's need, but not every man's greed." It is important to understand your prospects needs. This is the statement you are striving to hear: "You know, until we met today I didn't realize how unhappy I was with our current situation. Meeting with you has been very helpful."

The temptation at the end of any call is to close the deal, especially if the prospect has given you an opening like the statement above. "Sell now!" is what our culture has preached for many, many years. Alternatively, salespeople are told "if you feel uncomfortable during your meeting, just throw some amazing product features at your prospect and be sure to explain the awesome benefits of dealing with your company."

However, there might be a better way to establish a sales relationship than attempting to close the Gatekeeper or any other buyer during the initial meeting. Unless the prospect specifically asks that you present during the first meeting, approaching it as a fact-finding mission will enable you to listen more carefully without the temptation to hijack their stories. This especially holds true if your probing doesn't elicit any obvious pain from the prospect. The prospect may actually be happy with their current boyfriend. However, due to selfish motives, like the desire to win at all costs, I have experienced some very stupid attempts to impugn a competitor's integrity or pricing:

- "We beat our competitor's pricing by 15 percent every time."
- "How do you know that you aren't paying too much for the services they provide?"
- "Your vendor has been cheating you, and we can prove it."

While the last quote is extremely harsh, I must confess I was once party to an indictment of that sort. Our competitor was cheating the customer, and we could prove it. However, the result wasn't quite what we anticipated.

The prospect fired their supplier and then told us we were no longer welcome in their building because we were rude for exposing our competitor's failings. For a while, this prospect's attitude stumped our sales team. However, with some reflection, the incident confirmed that exposing the boyfriend as ugly or a cheater doesn't drive a prospect into your arms.

IF YOU CAN'T IDENTIFY ANY PAIN, DIFFERENTIATE

So, what can you do if you're unable to identify any discernable pain in your prospect? First, you must evaluate whether it is time to move on. Too many sales people fixate on selling to a company that may never buy from them.

Consider asking the prospect "What do you recommend I do?" Your honesty will likely differentiate you from the others and could lay the foundation for future conversations when they're looking for a new boyfriend. If they tell you that they're very satisfied, ask them if it makes sense for you to follow up periodically. Not winning today doesn't mean you won't win them over down the road. Always remember that, depending upon the product or service you are selling, they may not trust you enough to share their deepest needs—yet.

It's also possible they may not understand improvements and advancements in technology that companies in your industry can provide them. If their current boyfriend hasn't offered one of those "revolutionary" tools to their customers, you might be able to create a need. Once you have established your future relationship with them, you can offer them a quick synopsis of the available high-tech solutions in your industry.

In the office products field, two web-based programs are currently available that buyers and especially purchasing agents can use—if they're introduced to the technology. All vendors within the office products industry have access to one of the programs, but operating it is downright scary. The customer can easily view all of their products and prices in near real time, which could enable the purchasing agent to compare other vendors without any input from the incumbent's sales team. Consequently, most office products dealers do not introduce this product to anyone. However, many creative salespeople have discovered that it can create pain where none existed earlier. I have participated in numerous calls where this product was introduced to buyers who had no issues with their boyfriend. A few of the prospects almost began drooling with excitement when they understood the control this tool gave them.

But, whatever follows from introducing a controversial tool like this, do not verbally throw the prospect's current vendor under the bus. Just let the buyer evaluate the fact that you brought this amazing product to them. In fact, it is important to add the caveat, "I am sure your current vendor [boyfriend] meant to introduce it to you, and if you ask them, they will provide it for your company at no cost."

Does your industry provide a similar data-mining product that you are afraid to offer. Could you introduce it to potential customers who may not exhibit any other concerns with their current supplier? Do you have other tools to differentiate your company without lowering the price, diminishing your profits, or reducing your value to the customer?

The other product in the independent office products world provides a solution that most competitors can't duplicate. It systematically analyzes a customer's usage in order to determine if the dealer could sell them other products that would lower their overall expenditures. It simultaneously evaluates the products to determine which ones would save the customer money while improving the dealer's profitability.

In a business where tens of thousands of products possess a similar fit, form, and function, a tool like this is unbelievably powerful. Sadly, dealers who possess the tool rarely use it and almost never introduce it to prospects. But they push their salespeople to raise margins and close new accounts on a regular basis.

Going back to the premise of chapter 3, do you see how the tools and techniques like the two listed above could enable you to sail out of red oceans where price is king into a blue ocean that adds exceptional value to your prospects? Is anything comparable in your type of business?

Perhaps others have overlooked or wouldn't consider introducing a valuable tool specific in your industry to a prospect. Utilizing something that differentiates your company from other competitors is the key to making confident next steps towards beginning a sales relationship. Rather than starting at a +1 on the loyalty scale indicating the beginning of a buying relationship, generating creative solutions will enable you to start the new sales relationship at a higher trust level, like +4 or +5.

ASKING FOR THE NEXT STEPS

Assuming you have identified a few pain points that your company can address or even some issues that you have made them aware of, your next step is to summarize what you discovered and then solicit their acceptance of your summary. Did you understand how they ranked their challenges from least important to most important? If you are receiving positive comments from the prospect, you need to ask the Gatekeeper or buyer for guidance on next steps. You could say something like this:

> It is approximately 3:45 and we scheduled our meeting until 4:00. We could spend the rest of our time discussing some ways our company may be able to address the problems you are facing—or should we schedule a follow-up meeting so you won't be rushed for time?

While many salespeople might say, "Don't forfeit this opportunity to wrap it up! Find a way to close them now, or you'll lose them for good." Alas, I disagree about closing at any cost. The process I have outlined so far is methodical and designed to establish an *actual* relationship. So if you have discovered previously unidentified needs or provided value to them by listening, they may want to buy from you no matter when you close. A few days ago a rep asked me how to avoid chasing down the prospect for a second meeting or a decision. In my experience, setting the second appointment has been easy as long as the sales professional intrigued the prospect during the first meeting.

As I explained at the beginning of the book, the prospect knows you are a salesperson and yet if you haven't tried selling them anything but sought to understand them and their challenges, they will likely ask to extend your current meeting so you can discuss possible improvements for their company, or they will set a time for a follow-up meeting so you can present your solutions.

However, if they say something like, "We can't go past four o'clock today, so please call me next week to schedule a follow-up appointment," they either don't have their calendar with them or they didn't find value in your time together. In either case, you must challenge their response.

AT THIS POINT IN THE RELATIONSHIP, YOU DO HAVE RIGHTS

This is the first instance in which I recommend that a salesperson become persistent in their pursuit of a clear direction from the prospect. Humbly listening to others and doing your best to understand their needs does not imply that you have no rights. Time is your most precious resource. So if you invest thirty to forty-five minutes in a discovery session, you have earned the right to present or at least know the reason why they don't want to meet again.

> Humbly listening to others to understand their needs does not imply that you have no rights.

Sandler sales training suggests that you never allow prospects to "think it over" and even to get the prospect to agree to not resort to the "think it over" argument at the end of the call. As part of an upfront contract with the prospect Sandler suggests that you ask for a "yes we can meet again" or "No, we don't have a need for your service at the present time." I couldn't agree more, but having been in this situation a number of times, asserting your right to clarify next steps without offending your prospect can be difficult. So I suggest you employ a specific methodology to ensure that (1) you don't chase a prospect who really isn't interested and (2) you are not relegated to "just another sales rep" status with the prospect.

If you are nearing the end of the allotted time and haven't discussed ways that you might alleviate some of their pain, or the prospect won't schedule a specific time for you to present your findings, then it's time to employ the "going for the no" or "reversing" strategy:

> Jane, I want to apologize. It sounds like I misunderstood the importance of the challenges we discussed to your company. I hope you don't

feel that I wasted your time. Should we suspend our discussions at this point? You can contact us if you have any further interest in our product/service. How does that sound?

This strategy is the single most powerful tool in a salesperson's arsenal. You can use it to discover how little or how much they valued the meeting. Alternatively, if they are intrigued by your approach or your personality, they will reveal how they feel and what the next steps should be. It also establishes that as a professional, you are too busy to waste time chasing buyers who cannot provide a simple yes or no answer about next steps.

"Actually, we *are* very interested in understanding how your company might be able to help us with the issues you described. However, I am very busy the rest of this week and my calendar is on my phone in my office."

"Could we set a couple of tentative times for next week and then you let me know by tomorrow morning which one works best for your schedule?"

"Sure!"

"Thanks again for meeting with me today."

HOW TO SET UP THE NEXT APPOINTMENT AFTER A NEGATIVE RESPONSE

Here's how to respond if the prospect seems negative, disinterested, or disengaged:

"We are interested in talking more, but we're very busy right now. Could you send us some pricing so we can evaluate your company against our current vendor?"

"Thanks for letting me know your thoughts. I am afraid that if you're only looking for lower prices, we'll disappoint you. We're very competitive but we differentiate ourselves by proactively saving our customers time, while enabling them to be more efficient. If you're just looking for competitive prices, my guess is that your current vendor [boyfriend] is already doing a good job."

"How can we know you're competitive if you don't provide us with some pricing? We need to know that switching from our current supplier to you will save us money."

"Again, I apologize for any misunderstanding. I believe we can save you money by dealing with the issues you described during our meeting. We're also willing to guarantee in writing that our pricing will be at least as low as your current suppliers for a three- to six-month trial period or we'll refund the difference. However, I planned on introducing that guarantee during our presentation, because it isn't the main reason you should consider switching your business to us."

"We cannot meet any further unless you guarantee you will beat all of our current vendors' prices."

"I understand completely, and since we can't commit to that in good conscience, I wish you and your company all the best."

Both scenarios are wins. The positive interaction is definitely more exciting because you can potentially move the prospect to a +1 or even +4 after the next meeting. However, the second exchange also has potential. Total honesty with anyone, especially a prospect, is the most freeing feeling a salesperson can experience. The negative prospect may never buy from your company, but they will always respect you for declining the opportunity to move forward based purely on price. They could also come back when they run into real trouble with their boyfriend. Moreover, you are fully justified in deleting them from your list of prospects or at the very least preventing yourself from wasting precious time chasing their business any further.

Is all this effort worth it? The selling process I have suggested does not generally turn -13 prospects into +1 to +4 customers overnight. But, if we're honest with ourselves, we know that no shortcut exists to building lasting sales relationships. That is, unless the prospect's pain is so acute that they mention it to you during the first or second call. Can we admit that this doesn't happen often and quick closes are a mirage?

> Total honesty with anyone, especially a prospect, is the most freeing feeling a salesperson can experience.

Too many sales people have failed in sales because they tried to push toward the quick close. This tragic situation has ruined lives and caused prospects to hate the entire sales process. In the next chapter I'll describe the opposite of the ABC close. From long experience, I promise that properly crafting and presenting your company's proposal will bring great personal and financial reward.

CHAPTER 9

SELECTING YOUR NEW CUSTOMER

George Washington once said, "It is better to be alone than in bad company." He was right.

After uncovering two or three pain points with the prospect, you can have some fun!

Obviously, there are positives and negatives to presenting immediately—and you shouldn't ask to address their issues if you aren't able to provide complete answers. However, if listening to the prospect has caused them to *feel* the pain, presenting immediately is preferable as long as they ask for you to continue the meeting. "Jane, it sounds like fixing the problems with your current product [or service] could really make your life easier. Would you like me to present some solutions now or schedule something with you and your team later this week?"

"Why don't you give me a quick synopsis of how your company could fix it and if necessary, we can set a more formal meeting later this week."

Remember to begin with the strongest argument that addresses their deepest pain and then move outward to other less dynamic pains.

Also, if you approach the prospect as if you have a million dollars in your back pocket like I described in chapter 6, you won't seem pushy or desperate. Even while you explain your solutions, asking questions and checking for acceptance ensures your prospect's continued engagement with the process:

"You said that your company struggles with cost overruns and sticking to a budget in this category. We provide a budget management system controlled by whoever you designate, so your employees never spend more on our services than their budgeted amount. Assuming that it works as I have described, would that address some of the challenges that you are struggling with?"

"Wow! That would make a big difference. Tell me how it works."

Patiently spend as much or as little time solving their pain as *they* direct. Remember to follow their lead on the call. Once they seem to thoroughly understand the first point or have minimized its importance, ask permission to address their second need:

"But I am really concerned about the pricing. We must have the lowest cost possible."

VETTING THE CUSTOMER

I entitled this chapter "Selecting Your New Customer" to address this type of challenge.

A few days ago I met with a prospect who complained about her current vendors, asked for some assistance with her process, and stated that she needed the lowest overall price. We did our best to understand her needs as thoroughly as she would allow and then asked for an opportunity to present.

After giving us permission to tell her about our company, she immediately jumped right into our biggest weakness. "Of course, I am looking for the lowest price." She also gathered invoices from our competitors and attempted to hand them to us for an evaluation.

As we discussed, anyone who claims to have the lowest prices all the time is either lying or offering such a revolutionary product or service that they don't need a sales professional to sell it for them. The company I represented is competitive but will never be the cheapest.

> Anyone who claims to have the lowest prices all the time is likely lying.

So, along with the saleswoman who accompanied me on the call, we addressed this weakness head on.

"Obviously, the lowest price is very important to you," I said.

"Yes," she replied. "We always need the lowest price possible, which is why I wanted to provide you with our invoices—so you could compare them."

"Thanks," I explained, confident of the million dollars in my back pocket. "But if you're only looking for the best price, maybe you should stay with your current supplier. We don't feel comfortable looking at our competitor's pricing because we wouldn't want our customers sharing our pricing with our competitors. Also, does a single vendor truly offer the lowest price on every product in the marketplace? We don't provide the lowest price on everything and I'm sure no one else does."

The tables had turned and now we were in the process of customer selection. From experience, I knew that if she only cared about the lowest price, her values wouldn't match up with ours. The next few seconds of the meeting became the win or lose moment. If she didn't understand or believe in our values, the meeting and our opportunity (at least at that time) would be over. Alternatively, if she appreciated the honest reversing that we exhibited, the account would be won without a guarantee of the lowest price.

"No, there isn't any one vendor that provides the very lowest price on everything," she admitted. "I just want to be sure that you are competitive."

Her answer enabled us to continue with the selection process and discuss her other areas of pain.

"We understand that you need competitive pricing, and we can provide that. However, you also stated that you are 'buried' at the present time and would like to streamline the process of ordering. Your current providers are unresponsive or don't provide any personal service. Is that correct?"

"Yes," she replied. "Every day we hire new people who I am responsible to train. Our company has also expanded from one location to multiple plants throughout the northwest. I can hardly see straight because of all the activity. Outsourcing this responsibility to someone else like your company would be a *huge* relief."

"We want to be sensitive to your time," my associate said. "What if we commit to matching your overall costs for three months with the understanding that you will purchase only from us during that time? At the end of that period, you can compare our invoices to your current vendors and if we aren't the same price or lower overall, we'll refund the difference."

"That sounds great."

My associate continued: "I am willing to take care of any immediate needs right now and provide you with my cell phone number to expedite our conversations. We will also streamline your processes as I become more familiar with your company. Between now and then you can call or e-mail me with any emergencies and by next week everything should be set up. How does that sound?"

We won!

THE VALUE OF A WRITTEN GUARANTEE

We "selected" a new customer that day and the customer selected us. But what about the guarantee?

Do we really want to commit to honor the current pricing from a competitor, sight unseen, with a written guarantee?

Yes, I do believe that providing a written guarantee is valuable for numerous reasons.

1. If a prospect doesn't believe there is any major difference between suppliers, the price commitment is a risk-free way for you to show off your services.

2. If you don't know how to price a prospect, and they only judge you by your quote, your chance of winning drops significantly.

3. By accepting your guarantee, the customer is admitting that they have other needs besides price.

4. In many cases, great service along with the perception of competitive pricing during the trial period will result in the customer feeling so good about you that they won't even compare you to other companies after the trial period.

5. Most competitors will accept other's invoices. Consequently turning down the request to examine other's priced invoices will set you apart as it did during our call.

6. Most competitors won't think of providing a simple solution like a price guarantee.

7. You won't need to prepare a formal presentation or proposal nor will anyone need to spend hours preparing completely customized pricing for the prospect.

Obviously, not all presentations go as well as the one I described in the last section. So keeping an open mind about whether a prospect is worth selecting will be a key to closing more business and maintaining your sanity.

NEVER UNDERESTIMATE THE POWER OF THE REVERSE CLOSE

I cannot overestimate the power of the reversing technique when meeting with prospects. For example, what if the prospect hasn't shared any pain and you haven't been able to discover any? Many sales professionals push forward anyway by attempting to embarrass the current boyfriend. If, after probing, you can't identify any significant pain, why not state this fact to the prospect?

"You know, it just doesn't seem I can offer you anything different from your current vendor. I would love to do business with your company, but if you don't feel we can improve your current situation, maybe we should just end the meeting here. What do you think?"

They may thank you and agree that nothing further can be gained. But they may also fight the notion that you can't solve their needs and bring up other pains or improvements that they perceive your company could provide. But you will never know until you ask a reversing question. You might be surprised when they respond with something like the following:

"On the contrary, I am really intrigued by your company. You haven't approached this process like anyone I have ever dealt with. It is refreshing to feel that someone isn't just trying to sell me. Could we talk some more?"

> Reversing is a powerful tool when you are closing a call after identifying and addressing their pain.

Reversing is also powerful when you are closing a call after identifying and addressing their pain. The prospect might have even expressed interest in trying out your services or products. Just beginning the process of closing the call may move them towards agreeing to specific next steps. I like to ask:

"So do you think the solutions we have presented might make a difference for your company? Because if I have misunderstood their importance to you I wouldn't want you to go through all the hassle of changing suppliers."

Nobody (or very few people) are this honest, but wouldn't you rather know whether they have any second thoughts before you begin integrating with the prospect's company?

The truth is that prospects and customers lie—a lot—most often because they don't want to hurt your feelings or they feel uncomfortable with confrontation. But this lack of forthrightness frustrates everyone in sales. Consequently, doing your best to validate their true feelings about the process will save you time, and thus money.

"Actually, I am thrilled with what we discovered today. It sounds like your company can really make a difference in gaining efficiencies for our team. So when and how do we start?"

If the prospect says something like this, congratulate yourself. You have won a new customer who is ready to move to the positive side of the loyalty scale. They want to buy from you, and as long as your company transitions their business quickly, you have become a new boyfriend.

You'll discover great personal and corporate benefits through using this method to sell. Selling with an honest approach promotes loyalty, while eliminating the need to deceive your prospects and customers about your weaknesses. We will discuss the power of honest selling in chapter 10. It will enable you to sleep better and differentiate your company from most of your competition.

CHAPTER 10

SELLING HONESTLY

"What are words for, when no one listens anymore?"
—From "Words" by Missing Persons
(1980s Punk Rock band)

"Do you like it when other people try to sell you something the minute you meet them?"

"Do you attempt to entice more than 50 percent of your prospects by leading with price?"

"Do you believe that your product or service will actually save your prospect money over time?"

"Do you chase prospects longer than you should because it feels less threatening than finding new prospects?"

Within the last few weeks, I asked professionals from three sales organizations these questions. While establishing unanimity among different sales teams is difficult, in every case their answers to the above questions were, "No, Yes, No, and Yes."

Albert Einstein reportedly said, "Insanity is doing the same thing over and over, while expecting different results."

If we don't like it when people sell to us, then why do we repeatedly fall into the same sales trap? Could we salespeople actually be insane? If we don't move away from the red oceans described in *Blue Ocean Strategy,* we just might be certifiable.

Do you want to change? It's time for you salespeople and managers to reconsider your sales strategy.

HONESTY REALLY IS THE BEST POLICY

Building relationships without attempting to pitch a process or product is the first step toward selling honestly and effectively. How many times has a prospect said to you, "Thanks for coming by today. I look forward to seeing you again"?

The young lady I described in chapter 9 actually said this to my colleague and me as we prepared to leave her office. She even e-mailed the sales woman the next morning to ask more questions about how to engage with us. Unusual? Yes, but it shouldn't be that way.

Honesty in sales is refreshing. Who isn't looking for knowledgeable, personable resources to trust? The controversies surrounding fake news have made everyday people mistrust most news organizations in the same way that prospects attempt to avoid all sales professionals, because they have been turned off by dishonest sales pitches.

The three most important questions you can ask yourself with respect to growing your business are:

1. "Do I like my current process?"
2. "Does it match up with my value system?"
3. "Is it working as effectively as it could?"

Please notice that the most important part of this self-reflection lies in determining whether or not your sales process eats away at your integrity. Remember the car salesman I mentioned in chapter 4? His sales successes led him to become a person that to this day scares me to when I think about him. According to M. Scott Peck's definition of evil in his revolutionary book *People of The Lie*, the car salesman tried to entice me into a life of manipulation that would have made me become evil.

Peck states, "Evil is Live spelled backwards."

There is no one more alive than a salesperson providing a product or service that can help individuals and companies become more efficient or effective. But that same salesperson could become so successful or unbelievably discouraged that they begin to allow the ends to justify the means. Success becomes their god and customers are just the means by which they win. That sort of attitude is evil to its core.

Could it be that a salesperson either moves toward being more honest or more narcissistic during every call? I believe this assertion is true—which means our conduct at work affects our personal lives and our character. The 1980s punk rock band Missing Persons wrote a song called "Words" that began "Do you hear me? Do you care?"

> A salesperson either moves toward being more honest or more narcissistic during every call

If we are selling to people, and everyone has intrinsic worth, isn't making on honest attempt to connect at a personal level vital to our own well-being as well as creating a sale?

The Missing Persons song goes on to suggest that the purpose of our words must change or the world that we live in will completely tune out. Are we there yet?

People desire to be heard while many salespeople desire only to sell. Selling honestly and effectively begins with a conversation based upon active listening. Active listening may be the most powerful blue ocean of them all. That is tragic because honest respect for another individual should not be that unusual. But often it is.

SELLING SHOULD BEGIN WITH RELATIONSHIPS, NOT PRICE

When you're dating the Gatekeeper, the goal is to create a relationship from nothing. By doing this you're also separating yourself from the other salespeople who the Gatekeepers encounter. Consideration, sensitivity, and concern for the well-being of the person with whom you are interacting differentiates an honorable sales professional from a selfish sociopath. The goal of every cold call should be to make that person's day better without interrupting it significantly.

> Consideration, sensitivity, and concern for the well-being of the person with whom you are interacting differentiates an honorable sales professional from a selfish sociopath.

Once you have established a mind-set for creating relationships rather than just selling something to an unknown somebody, your reactions become more attuned to selling honestly. Salespeople sell the possibility of lower prices because they want the prospect to question their loyalty to their current boyfriend.

Wouldn't it be more intriguing to the prospect if you actually admitted the complete truth? "We do not have the lowest price and, by the way, who does? If that is all you are looking for, it makes sense for you to continue working with your current supplier."

Recently, a vice president for one of the larger businesses in the United States contacted me and asked if our company would like to bid for their business. Although surprised that someone from a company that big would take the time to contact me (we had never made a call on them), I was able to hide my excitement and get the facts.

They were unhappy with their current supplier, but he explained that price would still account for at least 60 percent of their decision. When someone mentions that price will color over 50 percent or more of their decision-making process, it might be more realistic to write the number down as 100 percent.

Right away I knew the prospect was unhappy and price was their most important variable. What do you do when you are presented with the possibility of making the largest sale in your history, but you know the decision will be based mostly on price? Fight for it? Spend a significant amount of your company's time pursuing a prospect that could put your company on the map, so to speak?

Not if you want to date the Gatekeeper. I turned down the chance to participate in their bid and then the conversation became interesting. The prospect was stunned.

"Why would you pass up the chance to sell tens of millions of dollars to a Fortune 50 company?" he asked.

I explained, "There's no doubt that your company has already negotiated extremely competitive pricing, so apart from not liking the service you have received, why would you even consider moving your business?"

A verse in the Bible says, "The truth will set you free." In some ways this phrase resembles Sandler's Millionaire concept because it suggests that if you tell the truth and lose a business opportunity, you'll still be better off than lying in an attempt to move a deal forward.

What happened next was shocking. My unexpected response to his offer made him realize that our company might be different than the others he was contacting.

> If you tell the truth and lose a business opportunity, you'll still be better off than lying in an attempt to move a deal forward.

"Are you sure your company would not like to be involved in this bid? Not many vendors reject the opportunity to do business with us."

He was absolutely stunned by my answer, and I could sense the frustration, and interest, in his voice. I replied, "Our largest competitors are engaging in a race to the bottom that we have no interest in joining. We are growing profitably while their top and bottom lines are shrinking. Why would we want to participate in such a disastrous activity?" I essentially asked, "Why do you want us to sail in "red oceans?""

At one time there had been five large competitors in our field, but bankruptcies, mergers, and lawsuits decimated our competition. Apart from our group of independents only two large companies were left, and price competition was deeply wounding both of them. I suggested that his company not go out to bid, because with the current state of our industry, their prices might go up.

Obviously, this was an unusual sales call. However, because I told him things he had never heard from a vendor, he became intrigued with our company. We have met on numerous occasions and engaged in far-ranging discussions about how they might utilize our services.

We haven't gained any business yet, but if their current boyfriend causes them too much pain, they will likely look to us first. And we will make money for the services we provide, rather than lose money by bidding for their business.

DIFFERENTIATING YOURSELF FROM THE COMPETITION

What about you? Does the product you sell and the company you represent differentiate itself in any other area besides price? Whenever you start a sales pitch with any variation of the phrase, "You will save lots of money" you have destined the relationship to sail in a red ocean. Not only that, but you will face the temptation to deceive them in one way or another.

Does your product or company have a specific value besides price? Consider the following questions:

Why should anyone buy from my company?

Why should anyone buy from me?

What differentiates our offering from our competitors besides price?

How can I help a prospect discover our value without leading with price?

Would I buy from my company and me?

You may not think it makes sense to write a chapter on why price doesn't matter. In reality, when we start discussing price with customers we are more likely begin compromising our values.

To be a high performing sales person in an unbelievably competitive sales environment, you must have an edge. Either you will represent the cheapest product or service on the face of the earth or you will cultivate relationships in order to understand the prospect's needs more completely than your competition.

The choice between these two paths might determine your long-term business success and the type of person you become. Choose carefully.

FREQUENTLY ASKED QUESTIONS

Sales is a constantly evolving, diverse process, so the following frequently asked questions are designed to minimize any confusion that might have occurred as you've read this book. Feel free to e-mail me (Tom@ DatingTheGateKeeper.com) if you have any questions about specific situations not covered here.

HOW DO YOU DATE THE GATEKEEPER ON THE PHONE?

First, we need to answer the question with a question. Are you using the phone to set up an in-person sales call or to sell your product or service remotely?

If you are contacting a prospect you will eventually see in person, the process is easy. Your only change from the in-person cold call involves establishing your business's location within the prospect's home area.

Admittedly, this sounds a bit more salesish than I prefer, but you must establish your purpose more quickly when you don't have the benefit of being there personally. I usually say something like this:

"Good morning, my name is Tom Buxton from Tom's Commodity Solutions here in Denver. And your name is? (Make sure to wait for their answer) I'll bet your company has a great insurance provider. Yes? Most people do. I just wondered, I am planning on being in your area tomorrow and would like to drop off a gift for you from our company. I promise I won't try to sell to you or anyone else. Is that's okay with you? Thank you, I will see you tomorrow."

Admittedly, if you are trying to sell your commodity remotely, the Dating the Gatekeeper technique can be very difficult. I recommend spending a significant amount of time on the company's website learning about the Gatekeeper and any other relevant decision makers. Your web search should also help you determine whether or not you want to pursue this company. If so, I would send a gift to the Gatekeeper and the decision maker ahead of your phone call, along with a note that provides valuable information about the product or service you provide. Again, I wouldn't include any enticing offers or specific pricing. Call and greet the Gatekeeper after an appropriate amount of time (usually a week or so has passed so you are confident they have received your gift. Hopefully, you can move directly to the second call.

WHAT SHOULD YOU DO IF THE GATEKEEPER IS BUSY WHEN YOU ARRIVE?

If the Gatekeeper is on the phone or speaking to someone when you walk in the door, sit down if possible.

If there are no chairs, stand as far as you can away from the person. Generally, they will know you are present and your reason for being there. If no one is in the front when you arrive, sit for up to three minutes and wait without checking your phone.

If the Gatekeeper continues to be busy after no more than five minutes leave. Make a point to see them again if you believe your product or service might fit their company.

WHAT IF THERE IS NO GATEKEEPER, JUST A PHONE OR DOORBELL?

That's a tough call. Some companies list the names and functions of their employees so you can contact the correct person. I'm usually tempted to contact a lower level person rather than immediately engage the potential buyer. However, whoever you choose to contact, thank them for answering and tell them the name of your company. Be sure to mention you are confident they don't need anything today, so you just want to leave them a gift.

If you encounter a locked door, you could also write down the company's name and call them later that day.

HOW DO I DEAL WITH A NO SOLICITING SIGN?

Walk into the office and say something like, "I am very sensitive to your "No Soliciting sign and I am a salesperson. Could I please set up an appointment with you on another day? I am sure that you are happy with your current _____ supplier, but I would like the chance to understand more about your company if that would be ok with you. By the way, would you like a purple pen? May I have your card please?"

WHERE DO I STAND DURING AN INITIAL CALL?

Sales reps often act like they own the room. Consequently, make sure you express your humility. Stand at a distance from the Gatekeeper until you offer him or her the gift. Then shake their hand. Be sensitive to the Gatekeeper's workspace. Never place your portfolio or notebook on the Gatekeeper's desk. Also be sensitive to their needs. Give them some privacy if their phone rings. Step away from their desk or sit down if it seems like they will be busy for a few minutes.

SHOULD I GIVE PURPLE PENS TO MEN?

Believe it or not, most men I have encountered love purple pens. When the first person I meet in an office is a man, I treat him the same as a woman. I state that they probably have a great supplier for whatever I am selling and ask if they would like a purple pen. I have never been turned down and many men have stated that they will give it to their wife or significant other. Isn't that awesome? If someone gives the gift you provided to someone important or significant, it solidifies a positive image of your interaction in their mind.

SHOULD I PARTICIPATE IN AN APPOINTMENT THAT LASTS ONLY FIFTEEN MINUTES OR LESS?

Two solutions: First, attempt to reschedule at a better time for them. In general, this will add less stress to the prospect while demonstrating your sensitivity to their needs. If the prospect still wants to meet, be sure to ask why. Ask what they would they like to accomplish in fifteen minutes and how they suggest the meeting should proceed. You might discover very quickly that they are hunting for something specific, often lower prices. If that turns out to be the only reason the meeting was originally scheduled, you can answer that question in a very concise manner.

ABOUT TOM

Since 1988, Tom Buxton has tallied tens of millions of dollars in office products sales. The sales division he led won numerous awards for sales performance and consistently maintained the highest margins in the company's twenty-eight branches.

Tom currently serves as the national sales manager for American Office Products Distributors and has consulted with numerous types of sales enterprises. He has successfully consulted with companies as varied as pool supply businesses and law firms. Tom is passionate about equipping owners and inspiring salespeople to win new business and create sales growth with prospects and current customers *without relying on price as the most important differentiator.*

As a popular presenter, Tom has spoken to groups of two to two thousand in venues from Las Vegas to the Bahamas. Sales folks love him because he avoids "Death by PowerPoint" and abhors boring lectures. If you want to learn more about how to compete in a tough sales environment and enjoy yourself at the same time, be sure to contact him at Tom@DatingTheGateKeeper.com. Tom lives in Littleton, Colorado with his wife Jennifer.

Tom Buxton
Tom@DatingTheGateKeeper.com
www.DatingTheGatekeeper.com

CPSIA information can be obtained
at www.ICGtesting.com
Printed in the USA
FFOW02n1953140318
45702451-46550FF